ATTORNEY *by* DAY,

Novelist

by NIGHT

Advance Praise

"If you think you want to write a book, or you have a book inside you burning to get out, then this is the book for you! Kim Benjamin has created a step-by-step process that reads and functions more like a magical framework for the creative process than a boring strategy; and she has carefully crafted fun exercises all along the way – to stimulate your creative juices and help you move into richer storytelling. I wish I'd had this author's companion when I wrote my first book!"

—**Jackie Black**, PhD, BCC, author of *Love Like a Black Belt: Cracking the Code to Being a Happy Couple*

"In her book *Attorney by Day, Novelist by Night*, Kim Benjamin wraps her loving arms around you with a sweet combination of 'I get you' and 'You can do it' that pulls you in and makes you truly believe. This book brings to the forefront the idea that your thoughts create your reality. And that getting your book out to the world requires working on the inside of you. And that's where this book takes you, on a wonderful journey of exploration and discovery of *you*. She offers exercises that are as interesting as they are realistic, each one building on the next to gradually lead you to fulfilling your dream of writing a book. Filled to the brim with motivation and inspiration, this is a must-read for anyone who longs to write the book (and live the life) they've always dreamed of."

— **Jennifer Powers**, MCC, author of *Oh, Shift*

ATTORNEY *by* DAY, Novelist *by* NIGHT

Bring Your Book to Light
While Still Practicing Law

KIM BENJAMIN

NEW YORK

NASHVILLE • MELBOURNE • VANCOUVER

ATTORNEY *by* DAY, *Novelist by* NIGHT
Bring Your Book to Light While Still Practicing Law

Published in New York, New York, by Morgan James Publishing partnership with Difference Press. Morgan James is a trademark of Morgan James, LLC. www.MorganJamesPublishing.com

The Morgan James Speakers Group can bring authors to your live event. For more information or to book an event visit The Morgan James Speakers Group at www.TheMorganJamesSpeakersGroup.com.

ISBN 978-1-68350-319-4 paperback
ISBN 978-1-68350-320-0 eBook
Library of Congress Control Number: 2016917884

Cover Design by:
Rachel Lopez
www.r2cdesign.com

Interior Design by:
Bonnie Bushman
The Whole Caboodle Graphic Design

Front Cover Art by:
Heidi Miller

Editing:
Grace Kerina

Author's photo courtesy of:
Jeffrey Reese Photography

In an effort to support local communities, raise awareness and funds, Morgan James Publishing donates a percentage of all book sales for the life of each book to Habitat for Humanity Peninsula and Greater Williamsburg.

Get involved today! Visit
www.MorganJamesBuilds.com

DEDICATION

This book is dedicated to my son, Zack,
for his constant inspiration and the joy I
feel in being his mother. He is my "why."

TABLE OF CONTENTS

HELLO, DOROTHY, AND WELCOME TO OZ

*"We must be willing to get rid of the life we planned,
so as to have the life that is waiting for us."*
—Joseph Campbell

If you are an attorney, it goes without saying that you are intelligent, well read, most likely very well spoken, and good with a pen. You didn't grind out an undergrad degree and obtain a juris doctor degree just by wiggling your nose. You worked very hard to be in the position you are in life. It shows. But it came with a pretty hefty bill attached to it – not just the past days of sleepless nights and the dry mouth and sweaty palms of trying your first case in front of a jury. No, the cost has been even greater, hasn't it?

I am a big Joseph Campbell fan. Are you familiar with him? That quote that has floated around for years about following our bliss without fear and the universe "opening doors where there were previously walls" resonates with many people. He also has a theory that we (people) don't truly want to know the meaning of life as much as we are "looking for the experience of being alive."

That one really struck me. My bookshelves are lined with books – stacks of them cover my floors, and most available flat surfaces, to be honest. I once told my sister, an attorney and a notorious procurer of books, that I was not buying another book until I had finished every one in my house. She just smiled and said, "Yeah, how's that working out so far?" I had to laugh. She was right. I will never stop buying books.

Why? As it turns out there are many reasons. The obvious, of course, is that I enjoy reading; but on the other side of that coin is a deeper reason, because, just as Joseph Campbell suggested, I have been searching for the feeling of being alive most of my life. That may sound a bit strange, to look for life in a book, but bear with me.

Looking back at my childhood, from the moment I could read, I consumed biographies of famous – even notorious – individuals. I was sure, somehow in my small, inquisitive child brain, that I would find the secret, the mystery to what I was supposed to do, who I was supposed to be, that magic key that unlocked all the doors of life.

That sounds pretty funny now, in retrospect, but as I look around my house, I see that although I put that notion away on a conscious level, somewhere hidden from my left-brain consciousness, it still lurks.

My shelves don't hold as many biographies now. Instead, they are loaded with more practical manuals. I have 20 books on how to write a book (yes, really), at least 15 on tapping into the creative juju inside. I have Frankl's *Man's Search for Meaning* and musings from Marcus Aurelias, C.S. Lewis, Julia Cameron, Emerson, Thoreau, Picasso, etc. But of all of these books, the only one that truly points out my purpose is a small, four-page, three-inch-by-five-inch "book" written on office notepaper and published by a "company" that has long since ceased to exist. The title is neither ominous nor earth shattering: *The Cat, the Dog, and the Horse*. It was written by Kim Bagley.

It was the first book I ever wrote. I wrote it at the ripe old age of five – I know that only from a note my mother made on the back of the book.

The story is a brief, but moving, saga about the plight of three animals, and their journey to freedom. No, that is not true. It is a four-page read, one sentence per page, with misspelled words and crude illustrations.

Why is that book so compelling? There are several reasons. One, because it points to that thing that I most enjoyed doing before I "learned" what I should be doing. And, for another reason, it was also, I believe, a sign that pointed the way for me for all these years in between – a sign I simply chose to ignore.

We moved seven times before I went to high school, and my mother was anything but nostalgic. If it didn't serve a purpose, it was disposed of. She had way too much going on to keep every sentimental trinket created by her children. My baby book was only partially finished, and there was one small box of photos of me as a child, mostly taken by my grandmother. I actually feel fortunate I have even those things, because neither of my younger sisters have a baby book at all.

The fact that my mother kept that simple item speaks volumes to me. She isn't around any longer for me to ask, and I didn't find my little book until after her death, when I saw it lying in a drawer of the desk at which she spent most of her last days.

That was eight years ago. At the time it was becoming apparent that I would soon be in the middle of a divorce. My only child was struggling with all of the pain that accompanies the tearing apart of a family. I had given up my career as an interior designer years earlier to go to work with my husband in the financial industry. *Finance* – not my strong suit, I might add. All of that meant I would once again have to redefine my life and take on a new role.

There was a lot going on, needless to say. But amid the grief, loss, and change the thing that most stood out for me was that I felt that my brilliant, talented mother had died an unfinished life. That was my definition. I'm not sure she would have described it that way. Living through her death, my stepfather's unexpected death shortly thereafter, the death of my marriage, and the anguish my son went through gave me the gift of awareness. As I looked around at all the things that had to evolve, what I kept going back to was the thought, "If I were dying right now, today, what would I feel the most loss over?" In other words, what had been the cost of the way I'd lived my life so far?

Apart from having more time with those I loved, all I could think of were the file drawers of unfinished manuscripts, novel ideas, character descriptions scribbled on envelopes, plot lines laid out on legal pads, character and setting images, and scraps of paper bursting out of file folders like flowers pushing up through the earth to reach the sun.

Finding my first little "novel" focused my attention on the questions in my mind as clearly and intently as a cat chasing a laser pointer.

Even after that revelation, however, it took me another seven years to bring that dream of what I really wanted to do to fruition. Seven years of stops and starts, doubts, rabbit holes, and, yes, even a trip to Oz – all in search of what was right there before me the whole time.

Why didn't I notice it sooner? Perhaps because it was so quiet, so innocuous, and so small that I dismissed it? Or that I did everything I could to deny its existence? I downplayed it, minimized it, told myself how ridiculous it was, that it was a pipe dream, that it was too late, that I was middle-aged. The years of creativity should have happened long ago. Why would anyone care? What difference would it make? How could I ever hope to eke out a living by doing something as crazy as write a book? Who was I kidding? But then I would think of my mother and her dreams of gardens, of making art, of the projects she never finished and the things she always talked about but never got around to. The voice just wouldn't go away.

This begs the question: what about you? What is that nagging voice in your head saying? You know, the one you try to ignore?

I understand how hard your life is. You can't just stop doing what you're doing to follow some dream, some "bliss," as Joseph Campbell called it, even if it is supposed to create magic when you do. You have a *real* life, real bills, real commitments, and real clients.

Still, I am curious about what goes through your mind each day as you filter through the lives of others, past and present.

What I am wondering is what made you pick this book up in the first place? Were you an English major in college, or perhaps a history, poly sci, philosophy major? I am betting your major was in one of the liberal arts schools of some kind, one that allowed you to read and write.

Why did you choose a broad liberal arts degree? Why not medicine? Why not education? Why not risk management, or any of the host of specific career paths? Do you ever ponder that question? Or do you already know the answer?

— — —

Does the following scenario sound at all like your days as an attorney?

Some days the wind is in your sails and you move ahead like Kate Winslet at the bow of the Titanic, arms spread wide taking it all in. The judge grants your motion and it is as if the salt air is misting your face with the grace of a gift. You hit every green light as you make your way to the office with the sun shinning down on you. Your client not only shows up on time for her deposition, but so do all the witnesses you called. The court reporter is efficient and cheerful, and opposing counsel has so few question it feels as if the case is all but won. Must be Leonardo DiCaprio at your back, holding you up. You finish much sooner than expected. Everything is tied up in a ribbon. You are confident and your exhilaration would match Kate's. Full steam ahead. You leave the office with the same enthusiasm you imagine she must have felt there on the bow of the boat. The day is beautiful and golden and all seems right with the world. "This legal career isn't so bad," you tell yourself, and your mind drifts back to that solitary defining moment when you decided to go to law school.

Studying law had not been your original intention when you entered undergrad. At that point you were 18 years old, bright eyed, fresh-faced and excited about life and the future. You dreamed of writing. Of living abroad. Of tasting everything life had to offer. But who really knows at age 18 what they want to do for the next 50 years, anyway?

You dove into college life and everything it had to offer. The ride was wonderful and, after all, college was not just about starting a career, it was that transitional step into adulthood.

The next four years flew by more quickly than you'd imagined they would. You arrived at senior year. Time to make an honest foray into a career. Law school presented itself as the perfect combination of practicality and skills usage. Reading, writing, research, defending the downtrodden – it all fit. And you knew that obtaining a PhD wouldn't pay off the student loans you had accumulated.

Law school was tough, the bar practically unbearable, but clerking for a very respectful attorney landed you in a wonderful, small firm and had you flying across the country on a private jet and learning more than you'd ever thought possible.

The stars were aligning and your dreams of writing at a quiet cafe in Paris seemed liked a long gone childhood dream. It was time to "grow up," you told yourself. *This* was the good life.

But then what happened?

Could it be that, just like Kate's short-lived euphoria, your years of practicing law were great until the boat hit an iceberg? It all began to crack in two and sink to the depths of the cold, dark Atlantic in the middle of the night.

Sure, your legal career kept you from drowning. Saved your life. Financially, anyway.

These days, however, you pore over cases to cite precedents for something you are working on. You wade through encyclopedia-size files of information to understand, assimilate, and apply. Your hours are tedious and long at times. The legal system often seems anything but fair and just. You question whether your client, although rightly deserving of a fair trial, is actually guilty of the things of which they are accused. And what about the prejudice of the supposedly non-prejudiced judicial? What about pouring blood, sweat, and tears into a case for three to five years only to have it all disappear with a singular stroke of the judge's pen?

Now that you have a firmer grip on reality and a clearer head, what's next? There is a hole in your heart. You have seen the other side of life and the course you charted so many years ago just doesn't fit anymore – not completely anyway. Sure, you can make it; you will make it. You won't die. You will go on to have new adventures, new experiences, new highs, but you are not the same person you once were.

What's more, you understand the pull of those road maps and the conversations between your characters that you hear in your head at odd moments. The ones that perhaps keep you from sleep. The ones that refuse to go away quietly. And now that you're aware that your old dreams of writing fiction haven't died, you also realize that you can't be the person you were when you first began practicing law.

That doesn't mean you are swinging out the life raft to jump ship and abandon your legal career, or that it was all for naught. You still value your work as an attorney. You still believe that you can and do make a difference. And you definitely appreciate it when you win your cases and the money flows in, right? It isn't all doom and gloom.

But I am guessing there is some part of you that knows you have more to say, more to share with the world. It is that part I want to help you with. It is that voice, that small but persistent voice which appears like tinnitus and refuses to go away that we are going to discuss. It is what caught your eye about this book and made you pick it up. Maybe, as you read through the description on the back, something made you think, "Well if she's doing this, why can't I?"

Nothing would make me happier than to walk hand in hand with you on this journey, to help you see, that yes, *you will write your novel*. You will not only write it, you will finish it, and it will be the most exhilarating, liberating experience you can imagine. It will change you in ways you cannot yet fathom. You will emerge from the experience a different person.

You will be able to stand on the bow of your new ship and toss that rare, exquisite, irreplaceable emerald necklace overboard. Why? Because you won't need it anymore. Once you tell your story you will feel free. The dream of becoming a writer will no longer be an elusive, haunting phantom. You won't want to hold on to the memories of what could have been. You will have the magic of what is.

Let's keep that excitement going.

Exercise for Enlightenment – Author Action Guide

In each chapter we are going to have some fun and so some very revealing exercises that will exorcise the demons that don't want you to find your dreams and live your life's purpose. We are going to begin with the **Author Action Guide** – a way of calling forth your inner muse.

Part 1:

For this exercise, go to your favorite stationery supplier, art store, or online resource (although beginning this exercise before reading Chapter One is very helpful, so find something near at hand at least to start). Find a journal that resonates with you. It might be a simple leather sketchbook from Barnes and Noble; an ornate, artfully illustrated book from a great source like Papaya; or something of your own creation. It is very important that this book is yours. It is important that it speaks to you on several levels.

I have a great blank-paged book that looks like a law book. I also gave one to my sister, who is a writer and a lawyer. I found it at a local shop. Take a little time to find something that makes you smile when you pick it up.

The work we do in this exercise is written out longhand. You will write your book on the computer, most likely, but the writing for this exercise needs to be done the old-fashioned way.

Now, here is the interesting part: you are going to turn your book sideways so that you write in it in the landscape direction. This may feel awkward at first, but just go with it. (My sister freaked out. She hated this idea.)

This book is your Author Action Guide. You will use it for writing the exercises in this book.

On the first page of your book, write your name, the date, and an agreement with yourself, one that you are willing to sign and that you intend to keep.

For example: "I, (your name), promise myself that I will spend 30 minutes a day writing in my Author Action Guide. I do this out of joy, not obligation. If I find myself growing frustrated with the exercises, I will take that as a cue that my inner voice needs to play for 15 minutes. I will not judge or berate myself. If I miss a day, for whatever reason, I will simply pick up where I left off and not try to go back and catch up. I am excited and fascinated to see where this journey takes me."

You can use that agreement or make up one that works better for you. This is your journey. I am just here to walk with you.

Every morning, preferably the first thing every morning, set a timer for 15 minutes, which means you might have to get up

15 minutes earlier than usual. Is your dream worth it? This is an important question to both ask yourself and to answer with complete honesty and clarity. Sit for a moment, if you need to, in order to get a gut-level, honest answer.

During those 15 minutes, write freely, stream of conscious, about something – anything. You will not stop to read, edit, or question what you've written.

It does not matter what you write. Just keep the pen moving.

When the timer goes off, stop. If you are in a flow and want to go for another few minutes this is okay, but preferably not more than five or ten minutes more, at the most. This is a simple way to get your monkey mind to slow down long enough for you to breathe and begin to connect more with your creative mind.

Part 2:

Part two of this exercise is to breathe. Nope, I'm not kidding. You may find that, as you are writing, there is an ugly gremlin called resistance that pops up. He (notice whether you think of that voice of resistance as male or female; or maybe it's your own voice) will try to convince you that this activity is a waste of your time and energy. "You could be sleeping, exercising, making coffee, doing any number of highly prized activities instead of this one. Besides, why the heck are you writing, anyway? It makes no sense."

That voice is the ego, whose sole purpose is to keep you safe. The only problem is that doing the same things and not risking or changing isn't really safe – it's just familiar. So ignore the voice and keep writing. And breathing.

At the end of the 15 minutes, take another minute or two to write down how you feel about the exercise. Do you feel spent, frustrated, annoyed, happy, energized? Whatever it is, try to find a few one-word statements that describe your emotions at the conclusion of the writing exercise every day. The only caveat is that there is no judgment of how you are feeling – only observation.

This 15-minute practice will be ongoing.

— — —

And that is it for now. Great work!

The small exercises and practices throughout this book may seem very simple. *And they are.* That is why they may also seem redundant, irritating, or non-productive. But they aren't.

For the moment, take a deep breath and allow whatever comes up to come up. Don't try to understand it, change it, or correct it. Just let it be.

If you find that you want to journal, in addition to the 15 minutes of stream of consciousness writing every morning, while using this book and going through the exercises, please do. Jot down whatever comes to mind. You will likely find it very helpful as you move along. If you do not want to journal, that is perfectly fine, too. Sometimes it's fun to keep a record of where we are, because it can later help us to see movement, but it is totally up to you. We are not trying to add more work to your already very full schedule. The key to deciding whether you also want to journal is to be gentle with yourself and listen for the answer.

There's a Buddhist saying: "The journey of a thousand miles begins with one step." You just took your first step, and that's awesome. Personally, I am smiling a really big smile, just for you!

Chapter 1

CREATIVITY:
A PRIMER

*"Those who dream by day are cognizant of many
things that escape those who only dream at night."*
—**Edgar Allan Poe**

That novel you long to write is what is left of you before you squeezed your spirit into a world filled with suits, courtrooms, and the progression of steps required to be successful in the legal profession. That yearning is who you truly are. Make no mistake – your dreams are calling to you. They are not some random, arbitrary, hocus-pocus sent out by fate to humiliate you. It is no accident that you harbor these desires.

At least a tiny part of you longs to share your voice with the world. You have slugged it out with opponents, judges, even the law itself; gone head to head with them, so to speak. It probably got bloody at times, on both sides. And yet, with all of the courage that takes, with all of the intelligence, with all of the skill and training, you haven't even stuck your toe into the water for the artist that lives inside you. Did it ever even occur to you to fight for that voice, the voice of your artist that still lives within you? If it hasn't, you aren't alone.

Take a Lesson from Children

Have you ever spent any time observing children? Apart from the ones screaming in the grocery store or crying in the movie, I mean. Children are fabulously creative because they haven't yet forgotten how to be. For them, purple polka-dot pants and an orange animal-print top seem just fine as a combination. Shoes that light up when they walk are necessary, not superfluous. Piles of mud and stone constitute a castle. And if their drawings don't take center stage on the refrigerator they question our taste and sanity, not theirs. I find those qualities fabulous. Even if you aren't a fan of small children, you cannot deny their sheer brilliance, fearlessness, and determination to be creative and true to themselves.

I remember all too well when my son was four. He climbed up on the kitchen counters and announced he was about to fly. He had just watched Peter Pan. I proceeded to explain to him that it wouldn't work. He looked me straight in the eye and said, "How do you know?" You got me there, buddy. How did I know?

I knew because I had learned about gravity, sometimes the hard way. I knew because I had learned about fear. I knew because the laws of nature had supplanted my imagination; and the weeds of doubt and disbelief had choked out my dreams and desires.

Fast-forward four years. My son took the shiny, blue spandex book cover I'd procured to preserve the resale value of his science book and re-appropriated it to something far more useful for his world. He placed it on his head as a do-rag because, after all, every good rapper needs one, *oui*?

The point is, he didn't care what my opinion was or what others might think. He believed he could fly. And what seemed embarrassing and ridiculous to me, such as wearing a book cover on his head, produced not a blip on the radar of his confidence back then.

Why?

My son was oblivious to gravity and the pressure to fit in because he still dreamed. He still allowed himself to be an artist. He believed in magic and music and laughter and the momentary bliss of living in the present. He was fully alive in the moment.

What happens to that magic when we grow up and become concerned with future events and "real world" requirements? It never leaves us, but – far too often – we pack it in a trunk and store it in the attic for another day, for a "someday." But is *someday* just what we tell ourselves because we feel we need to? Someday could be now.

Picasso was quoted as saying, "Every child is an artist. The problem is how to remain an artist once he grows up."

We are all born artists. Many would disagree with me, some vehemently. Far too often art is thought of as a lofty, otherworldly gift bestowed upon a lucky, chosen few. But we make our own magic. You weren't just born an artist, you *are* an artist.

Why should all of this matter to you?

Every morning, grace withstanding, you wake up and are embraced by a new day, a clean slate to draw upon. I don't know what your morning routine is, nor does it matter. You will move through a series of well-practiced activities until you get in your car to drive to work.

Most likely, you simply do all of that without self-observation. But have you ever thought to consider that for each move, every practiced habit, every item you use, what you drive, where you live – a decision was required? At some point in our lives we chose those things. We probably never thought of those decisions as a form of creativity, but they were. Of all the millions of choices you could make, something inside you, that very unique make up that is you, chose what you chose.

Take a moment to let this information sink in completely. And then ask yourself what motivated you into your current state of life? Getting down to the core, why did all of those dreams of long ago suddenly take cover? What keeps them safely locked away from view?

One of my favorite books on recovering the lost artist within is Julia Cameron's *The Artist's Way*. In it, she explains, in depth, what art is and what it isn't. Ironically (or is it), her findings coincide with that of Picasso's: we are all born creative beings. When we were young and unencumbered by the confines of societal typecasting, we created freely and with abandon. Everything was our canvas, our typewriter, our architectural design, our story, our stage, and our music. Nothing was off limits; nothing was too hard or impossible. If we couldn't get to what we wanted one way, we would try another. If our goal became too frustrating, we would simply change the color or the direction or the cadence – but we never stopped until we reached some form of satisfaction, or fell asleep (which we fought at every turn because we feared we would miss something wonderful).

What happened to us? Why couldn't we remain the artist of our birth?

I believe that somewhere along the way, the voices of *wisdom* told us to "grow up"? I italicize *wisdom* in deference to the adults who loved us and only wanted what they thought was best for us.

Were we told our dreams were silly or impossible? Were we told we couldn't or shouldn't pursue them? Or did we simply absorb doubt, fear, and brokenness through osmosis? What did we make *being a grown-up* mean?

Every day in the physical realm in which we live there is new awakening. In nature every day something is forever being born, created, planted, cultured, renewed or removed. The brightness of the day is then followed by the night, full of its own gifts – stars, the moon, the sound of crickets, breezes off the waters lapping the sand of the beaches. With so many amazing things at hand to see, smell, touch, hear, and inspire us, what was it that so frightened us that we became convinced we are not artists?

Maybe a better question to ask would be: "How do you define art?" Seth Godin, in his book *The Icarus Deception*, defines it this way: "Art isn't pretty…. Art isn't something you hang on the wall. Art is what we do when we're truly alive."

The pretext is simple and supports what Picasso said, that we were born to create. The problem is keeping that desire, that wonder, that courage as we grow up.

I shared in the Introduction that my own path leading to this book began when I was five. Like you, I tried to fit my child artist into a form recognizable and acceptable by the presiding rules of society. I did that because I was, well, afraid. Afraid of what it might mean to truly go after my dreams.

> *"We have been taught to believe that negative equals realistic and positive equals unrealistic."*
> **—Susan Jeffers**

I fought the voices of passion and "grew up." I went through all the regular stations of life. But, despite my maneuvering toward being a grown-up, I never stopped longing to create. I married, had a child, and quit my interior design business to go to work for my ex-husband.

Time went by. Occasionally I would churn out a day's worth of writing poetry, or make a trip to the library or bookstore. I would read things I thought I could write and then things that seemed so far out of my league I would congratulate myself for not staging a platform on which I was sure I would fail. But none of this truly squelched my desire to create.

This is what I discovered: *our dreams will continue to re-visit us until we listen to them.* We can do everything in our power to ignore and silence them. Or we can choose the alternative.

We can choose to listen to what our dreams are trying to tell us about who we are.

Which option is truly less frightening – being haunted or opening to what is already inside of you?

— — —

There can be both amazement and frustration in this creative awakening. For me, the process has been rather circuitous. As I began to listen to the things that made me happy and made me smile, things that made me lose a sense of time, I grew less tolerant of the things that stole my joy and more aware of the awe of daily life. I found less satisfaction in things externally and grew more tolerant of the internal demands.

For a brief time, I had the opportunity to return to college just for the joy of it. I chose to study art. Then life, as it is sometimes does, threw me a curve ball that required I go back to work full-time in order to support myself. Moving away from art again was the collateral damage. I was back in the work place full-time again. Back to being "grown up."

Interestingly, however, that brief foray into the academic study of art provided me with valuable insight. All along, I'd thought I was going back to college to study art simply because I wanted to. I believed it was the logical stepping-stone to transition toward being more creative. Yes, the sheer enjoyment of art was a part of it, but what I came to also realize was that I needed to "legitimize" my passions. I didn't believe I could call myself an artist unless I had some sort of parchment that declared I had passed a test. Having art professors give me homework meant I was required to paint and draw and write.

In essence, I treated my creativity as a job. I realized then that the dreams of the five-year-old me hadn't disappeared, but the grown-up in me was still trying to keep her from jumping off the kitchen counter to see if she could fly.

After years and years of self-examination, a career, a child, marriage, I was still fighting the voice inside. I was still labeling and demonizing it. Why?

Maybe this isn't what you've been doing and you don't see yourself in much of my story – but I am betting some of it resonates. I could be wrong, but something made you pick up this book. Something called to you, the inner you, the wise you, the creator you. Maybe you've started a novel, but keep putting it aside, waiting for the times you 'feel' creative. Do you tell yourself it's just a hobby, something to pass the time? Is that really true?

I don't want to use the worn out adage "life is short," but it is. You have most likely spent decades of your life getting to where you are. You're proud of your accomplishments, as well you should be. You sacrificed a good bit to get here. But what do you want the rest of your life to look like? What calls to you? What creative passions do you only indulge in when you're at home alone, keeping it secret from the rest of the world, lest they tell you, once again, to "grow up"?

Here's what Julia Cameron has to say on this subject in *The Artist's Way*: "We… pretend it is hard to follow our heart's dreams….Turn aside your dream and it will come back… "

Listening to the things that bring life into your soul is the most grown-up thing you could do. Committing to what Julia

Cameron refers to as our "Africas, those dark and romantic notions that call to our deepest selves" takes courage, belief and persistence. But you have already demonstrated you have those qualities as a lawyer. You face the dark, romantic notions of championing your clients' causes every day. What if you took that same ability and belief and persistence and applied it to something besides your legal career?

What If You Indulged That Joy?
I believe as Julia Cameron (and Goethe and Louis Pasteur and W. H. Murray) – that if you decide and, even more importantly, commit, the universe will swing its magic doors wide open.

In order to do that, first, wrap your arms around yourself and truly embrace that wonderful, unique, fabulous part of you that you've tried to keep quiet for so long. It might prove challenging at times, frustrating, even hopeless. Just know that these stages you will go through are perfectly normal. They are part of the process of excavation. Much like with archaeology, years of debris – of being told or of believing that your dreams were unreachable or silly or far-fetched – will have to be gently but carefully swept away. It is not a journey for the faint-hearted, but then neither is life. To truly live your life, to find your purpose, is the beginning of hope.

> *"The cost of a thing is the amount of what I call life which is required to be exchanged for it, immediately or in the long run."*
> **—Henry David Thoreau**

At this point in our lives, many of us have exchanged a good portion of our life for our careers, homes, and families. The payment has been steep, but it has been a good investment. The question to ask now is, how great will the cost be should we decide to continue investing solely in the path we chose many years ago? How much will we "pay" in the long run if we choose not to accept that amazing creative being that resides within us.

Conversely, the only costs you absolutely must pay for on this journey of self-discovery is a willingness to see your own potential, to be open to the unknown, and to have compassion for the ride.

Reach into that child's heart that created out of sheer joy. Will you try? It is still there, I promise. It may be mummified with the years of "have to" and learned fears, but it still beats. It still calls to you. Are you willing to listen to it?

I realize I am asking a lot here. I am asking you to "dust off your soul," as Picasso said, to reconnect to who really are, not who you think you should be.

Your inner artist, your author ego, is most likely shy at this point, reticent to come out of the dark, much like a toddler who refuses to release its mother's hand. Our dreams seem fragile if we take them out of the box only occasionally to look at them. Bringing them fully into the sunlight may seem terrifying at first, crazy at best. But, much like the toddler eventually begins to see that he can step away from his mother just a little, we will begin to see how strong our dreams really are. We will see them bloom as we continue to encourage and support them. And, with the same compassion we feel for that frightened toddler, we will soon begin to appreciate the growth we are choosing to undertake.

You won't be alone. We will travel this together, you and I, through the minefields and quicksand and muggy rainforest haze. And you will come out the other side standing strong in your creativity.

Exercise for Enlightenment – Just for the Fun of It

In the Introduction, I asked you to get a journal or sketchpad and wake up a few minutes earlier in the morning to do freehand, stream-of-consciousness writing for 15 minutes. I hope you started and are continuing this practice and have begun to find hidden treasures within yourself.

Today, we'll add a little something to this practice.

This exercise can be done in two parts, and each part will take approximately 15 to 20 minutes to complete.

Part 1:

We are going to go future tripping. Imagine that you have released your novel and it hit *The New York Times* bestseller list and continues to stay there. *Really* allow yourself to take it in. What does your life look like? Are you going on book tours? Are you being interviewed on talk shows? What was it like when you received your first royalty check? Did you open a separate checking account? Did you invest in a new wardrobe for the promotional journey? Did you get a new hair style? What did your friends say? What did your family say? Was it everything you'd hoped and imagined?

Take 15 minutes and describe how your life has changed. It may be good or it could be not so good? How has it impacted you? How has it affected your career, your family, friends, and loved ones?

At the end of the 15 minutes, take another five minutes to give your current self advice, from that future place, from your future self. Look back from there to where you are now, knowing what you know then. What do you want to tell your current self?

Part 2:

As you write each morning, make note of anything special that comes up for you. Hopefully it will be good things, but it is okay if it isn't. Just jot down a few notes. You may be surprised that you are suddenly remembering your dreams at night, or that a conversation you unintentionally overheard would be a great story line. These are all signs that your creative muse is peeking out from behind the tree to she if she can come out to play. Invite her, take note of what she tells or shows you. Gently inviting that childhood joy back into your daily life will not only bring forth more of your author ego, it could suddenly make your days brighter as well.

> *"When you do things from your soul,*
> *you feel a river moving in you, a joy."*
> **—Rumi**

Chapter 2

PERCEPTION: THE STORIES WE TELL OURSELVES

"All that we see or seem is but a dream within a dream."
—Edgar Allan Poe

In 1849 Edgar Allan Poe published the poem "A Dream Within a Dream." The line above comes from that poem. In it, Poe struggles with the impermanence of reality. He reasons that if he can't hold a single grain of sand to prevent it from washing into the ocean, then there is no permanence and, therefore, he questions what is real and what is not.

More than 60 years after Poe wrote that poem, Carl Jung published his findings on the workings of the subconscious mind. In the Western world, Jung's concepts are still used to differentiate between the conscious, or rational, mind and the dreamy subconscious. Hundreds of authors, scientists, physicians, and academics have studied the brain to understand its complexity. Their consensus is that the subconscious mind does not distinguish between what is real and what is imagined.

I'll give you a couple of small examples of how our subconscious mind often regulates the outcome of our endeavors, whether we are aware of it or not.

There's been a shift in the way weight loss is discussed these days, with the word *diet* often replaced with *lifestyle change*, and with *losing weight* referred to instead as *releasing*. Why? Because the health and wellness industry is realizing that the term *diet* suggests a temporary condition, whereas *lifestyle change* implies health and an improved quality of life rather than a short-term goal of getting into a dress for a wedding or a high school reunion. The same is true for *releasing* weight rather than *losing* it. If we *lose* something, it indicates we hope to find it again. *Releasing* suggests we are choosing to let go of something that is no longer in our best interest to have.

Here's another example. I have a client with a master's degree who wants to branch out and start her own business, in that field. When we first began working together, she was adamant that she was not as qualified as her colleagues and peers. When I asked her why she thought that, she said it was because she hadn't really applied herself in school, but had just coasted through her classes. I challenged her presumption by asking her how many people she knew who had "coasted" through four years of undergrad and two years of grad school. She admitted that it didn't really ring true when she heard me state it like that. But that didn't change her belief immediately, because she had carried these thoughts around for years.

Whatever she believes is what she will hold onto. The same is true for all of us. Our *perceived* reality will, in essence, largely determine our reality. It seems redundant, doesn't it, that our reality determines our reality.

I am not suggesting that we can just think our way into utopia. I could cut out a photo of a Victoria Secret's model, glue it onto a poster board, and glue an image of my head on top of it. That doesn't mean I will wake up looking like that. If only it were that simple, right?

At the same time, perhaps in doing that I might shift my perception of what I see as possible and that might be enough to motivate me to increase my exercise routine or do a better job of eating healthy food. Maybe. The truth is a bit more complicated than that, but, at the same time, it's just as simple.

Throughout most of my early life, my artistic leanings went in the direction of the visual arts – drawing, painting, and mixed media. When I returned to college at the ripe old age of 40 to study art, it was primarily to study painting, not writing. My concept of myself and my interests and gifts did not include writing.

It wasn't until three separate incidents occurred within one week of each other that I even gave writing a second thought. I was nominated for a scholarship in literature and art history for my writing – which, in my mind at the time, I'd only done to serve my interest in art – and my mother, who had always been my biggest fan, casually mentioned that I was a better writer than I was an artist. Because I knew she loved me, I took that to mean I was at least average or above, in her view, with regard to painting, but a more effective artist with the written word.

That was revolutionary to me. Focusing on writing did not fall within the guidelines I had established for my life. It wasn't that I was opposed to writing. In fact, after giving it more thought, I recognized I had been writing all my life. But because I had not seen myself in that light, it came as a surprise to have my writing noticed.

It is not uncommon for us to see only one facet of who we are when we look into the mirror of our lives. Think of the stories you have read, or even people you know personally who are completely unaware of and perhaps even deny what you consider to be obvious. They downplay their abilities – not out of false modesty, but because they have never seen themselves in that light and therefore don't accept it.

On the other hand, there are artists, people in the public eye, leaders in industry, who seem to have more bravado than ability. But because they *believe* they have what it takes, they push their way to the top. How does that happen?

Any goal we undertake has to be framed within a certain belief to be attainable at all. The subconscious mind takes whatever we feed it and inputs it into its massive, complex database. From there, it processes and releases back to us thoughts that support our beliefs. This happens whether we are consciously aware of the process or not. The beauty and magnificence of the human brain is that it is at work all the time proving or disproving our beliefs as "reality."

That same force, the power of the subconscious mind, has been in effect in your life as well. Let me demonstrate.

I am guessing here, but doubt I am too far off. When you first entered law school, did you refer to yourself as an attorney? I imagine not. But, at some point, either during or after law school, you began to see yourself practicing law. Maybe it was in the mock trials conducted in class. Maybe it was after a particularly hard-fought test, or a paper that required several all-nighters in a row. Along the way, something subtle or not so subtle began to make its way into your thought process to allow you to see yourself as an attorney. *When* is not as important and *why*.

It has already been established that in order to succeed at your chosen profession you have to have a marked degree of intellect, or at least the ability to read, absorb, and regurgitate information on an above average level.

These skills, these gifts, these learned behaviors required you to shift your identity into that of someone who could perform the work needed for your chosen profession. This was critically important for your success and the benefit of your clients. The interesting part of this, however, is that learning to become an attorney and adjusting to calling yourself an attorney triggered a reality that may have over shadowed everything else you are.

I had dinner with my sister the other night. I asked her a question and she immediately went in to "lawyer mode." I laughed and when she asked me why, I said, "Because, wow, that was my attorney speaking, not my sister." She agreed and said, "Yes, I used to be a normal person. Then I went to law school."

The point is that going to law school and becoming an attorney was not only an avocation. It became your identity.

Who Are You, Really?

Think about the last time you went to an event where you were introduced to someone new. What was likely the first or second question after, "What's your name?" That's right. "What do you do for a living?"

And you probably answered, "I am an attorney." Not, "I practice law." Why? Because *being* an attorney is now an integral piece of who you are and how you see yourself. It is no longer something you *do* to pay the bills. It has become you.

This is a good thing, unless that part of your identity is so deeply ingrained that your conscious mind, the ego, refuses to let you believe that you can also do something else.

As mentioned above, the conscious mind, which is often referred to as the rational or left-brain, is what organizes and labels everything for us. It helps us remember directions to our house or office, understand contracts, and make non-emotional, logical, well-thought-out decisions. It is what allows us to function in the real world. Think of it as a super computer that assimilates data and spits it back out in order for us to get out of bed and get going every day. Much like autocorrect software, we run information through sequences to determine what we really mean. Just like autocorrect, it can turn one meaning into another, like turning one word into another.

The reason this matters so much is that, unless we are aware of this process and in control of our thoughts, the computer is much like an unruly child on the playground. It throws whatever it wills at us in an effort to keep the game of familiarity going. This means that *can't* literally becomes the default mechanism. Our super brains begin to come up with all kinds of rational reasons we can't do whatever it is that we think or believe we want to do, if it is outside our normal range of options.

So, say you decide to get those stories out of your head and down on paper. You sit down to your computer and happily begin to hammer out the story that has been creeping around in your brain for sometime. You work joyfully for an hour or more until, for whatever reason, you need to quit. All is well. You read back over the few pages we have written and are relatively surprised to see that it isn't all dog poop. You smile. You print it out and put the pages away with the intent to return to them the next day during your lunch hour.

The next day rolls around. Reading the morning paper with coffee, you notice there is a book review that looks pretty interesting, and the story is surprisingly similar to the story you were working on the night before. Intrigued, you decide that during the lunch break, instead of writing as planned, you will just run down to the bookstore and pick up this new book.

On the way back from lunch, the cell phone rings. It is a friend you were meeting for dinner. The conversation is brief, but as you hang up the phone, she mentions a book she is reading that she thinks you will just love. You tell her to text you the title of it.

Once back at the office you put the book and your lunch down on your desk and then remember the text from your friend. Amused, you notice she sent you the title of the same book. "Well, great minds think alike," you say to yourself.

You began to read the book. Ten pages into it, you feel as if you are reading the very same story you wrote just last night. Stunned, you close the book. There's no point in reading the rest of it, you tell yourself, you already know the ending.

You reach into your desk drawer, pull out the file folder with your manuscript in it and rip up the pages. You knew it was a ridiculous notion anyway, you tell yourself. Of course someone else has already come up with that plot line. Who were you kidding to believe otherwise?

Everything in you sighs in resignation and you pull out the file on the pending case you have been working on and hunker down to being an attorney.

Sound familiar?

This is the ego at its finest, the rational, logical part of the brain that wants to keep us safe; the voice of wisdom that doesn't want us to jump off the kitchen counter and go splat.

It feels safer to remember that you are an attorney, and a good one. You don't need to write a book, you tell yourself. You don't need to do anything but what you are already doing. You're already doing a good work. You have the potential to change people's lives. All of that is true.

But the old tapes that tell you being an attorney is all that you are run through your head on a loop, spreading with intensity like wildfire. They justify your decision to never try anything like that again. They tell you how lucky you are that you had not put any more blood, sweat, or tears into a doomed project. They tell you that they have your best interests at heart and are only thinking of you.

When you heed those thoughts, those voices, it feels similar to all the tragic love stories in the world. Rich guy falls in love with the girl from the wrong side of the tracks and they can't make it work, or debutante falls for truck driver and tragedy strikes. Heaven, hell, and their parents will all try to keep them apart – and succeed. Sometimes the consequences are dire; sometimes the result is a lifetime of disappointment.

As Henry David Thoreau said, "Most men lead lives of quiet desperation." The irony is that the desperation comes from listening to the ego over the subconscious. The ego's job is to keep the ship on an even keel and headed toward a familiar port... but sometimes one has to tip a bit to find the wind and reach the right destination.

The ego, what we come to believe is logic, is simply habit. Like the grooves that wear from years of walking the same path, some habits have become such a part of us that we have mistakenly fashioned them into a story, our story, the story of why we do what we do and why we can never change that. It isn't safe to change. Changing doesn't protect us. What we have is so familiar.

So, then, what to do? How do we change anyway?

It has been widely accepted for some time that our subconscious mind cannot distinguish between what is real and what is imagined. The things we consider facts are often contrivances to keep us from moving in a direction that might cause us to be uncomfortable or scared. Our logical brain simply cannot have that. Fear represents danger. Danger is to be avoided at all costs, even at the expense of joy.

The only way out of the darkness is to keep moving forward. We can't go around the uncomfortable, so we simply have to drive straight through the middle of it like a tank.

The good news is that this is where the fun starts. This is where we begin to understand and differentiate between our perception of what is and the story we tell ourselves about those perceptions. This is where we choose the story we want to write; and write the story we want to live.

Who Do You Want to Be, Really?

If you are anything like me, or the client I mentioned earlier, thoughts and ideas pop into your head at random times. You may stop to jot them down, put them into your phone or computer or leave yourself a voice memo. You capture thoughts as they come up.

But then what?

What happens to those recorded light-bulb moments? Those ethereal thoughts your inner wisdom floats in front of you to get your attention. What do you do with them?

I used to put them somewhere "for safe keeping" and promise to get to it later. Trouble was, I never did.

Why? Because my logical, rational brain was still trying to keep me safe. My brain kept reminding me that the work I was doing was far more important than some far-fetched notion about writing. I didn't admit that out loud, or even acknowledge it rationally, but if I were honest with myself that is what was happening. Not only that, if I needed more evidence I could talk to anyone who knew me and they would support the thought that it was better to keep going as I was than to try to do something different. They too saw me in the same light I had presented myself for years.

That's why I had file folders full of notes and file after file on my computer, 20 books about writing on my shelves, a computer program to help me write fiction, etc., etc., but mostly all it was doing was coming together in a great orchestration to keep my story real – the story I was telling myself to avoid moving into the darkness of the unknown.

Before I really took a leap toward my dreams of writing, I wanted evidence that I could succeed at it. But I wanted that before I began. I wanted to be assured of not failing before I took the risk. By telling myself it was too hard, or that plotline had been done before, I could avoid the darkness.

The darkness is scary because we don't know what's out there. We don't know what we might encounter. We want proof that we aren't crazy. That we have some talent.

Consider this: no one promised you that you would be a success as an attorney the moment you entered law school, and yet you did it anyway. There was a more calculated risk involved with law school, you tell yourself. If you applied yourself, if you were wiling to work ridiculous hours, study like mad, play whatever political game that came along, and keep your nose to the grindstone, you had sufficient reason to believe you would succeed. There was enough empirical evidence to prove that theory.

In creativity there is no such creature. It doesn't mater how much you invest, how hard you work, how many hours you put in or how many hands you shake, there is a greater than average chance you won't succeed.

So why do it?

Because everything in you knows you are called to try.

So, a better question is: "Why not do it?"

I have two quotes on my refrigerator. Well, truthfully I have a lot of quotes on my refrigerator, but I want to share two with you right now:

> *"Creativity, like human life, begins in darkness."*
> **—Julia Cameron**

> *"Do not fear mistakes, there are none."*
> **—Miles Davis**

Exercise for Enlightenment – Changing Direction

Understanding that the only obstacle standing between you and your novel is, well, *you*, is not a new concept. But the truth never grows old. Have you had enough of living the old story? If so, you are not alone.

So how does movement in a different direction happen? Good question. Here are a couple of exercises to get you started.

Part 1:

What is your dream within a dream?

What is that thing you think about on a regular basis but dismiss immediately from your mind as being unattainable or illogical?

Can you sit quietly for five minutes, close your eyes and picture it? It isn't important to figure out *how* it could ever come true. What is important is allowing your dream to come to life in your mind.

What does your dream look like? Where are you? What are you wearing? What is the temperature? What are you doing? Are you alone, or do you have someone with you? If someone's with, who is it? What time of the day is it?

Sink into the sensations of your dream. If you are on a beach somewhere writing, try to feel the sensation of digging your toes in the sand. Take another sip from your tropical drink. Feel the breeze off the ocean. Smell the sea and taste the salt in the air. Are you writing or just relaxing?

Getting into as much detail as possible, with as much sensory awareness as you can, will help to free your dream, and you, from the land of *never* or, worse *someday*.

Once you have a visual of your dream, write it down in your journal, or on your computer, with as much detail as possible.

If you find this exercise challenging, that's okay. It goes against your training as a lawyer and the work you do every day trying to prove or disprove things.

If you find this exercise frustrating, take a small break, set a timer for ten minutes, and get fully into your body. Turn on some of your favorite music and dance around the room or sing along. When the timer goes off, try this exercise again.

If you still find it challenging (or tedious), write down the thoughts are coming up for you as you try to do the exercise. What is the resistance about?

You can write whatever resistance comes up for you on a sheet of paper and symbolically destroy the paper, if you would like to.

You can repeat this exercise as often as you like. In doing so, you may begin to recognize the resistance more easily or quickly.

Release yourself from any judgment that may begin to surface, and be kind in the process. This will go a long way in making room for your dreams to grow. Notice the progress and note it in your journal if you would like. Pretty soon, your author ego, your internal muse, will feel the call to come out to play.

Part 2:
Recognizing your story begins with taking small steps. Write down every possible reason you have for *not* writing your novel. List everything that comes up – lack of time or resources, etc. – whatever springs to mind. Notice how you feel while writing this.

Then make a separate list of all the reasons you have to *finish* your novel. Again, write everything, no matter how small or insignificant it may seem, even if it's a reason like you will have more room in your desk drawer. Notice your feelings here.

Look at the two lists side by side. Which one is longer? Why do you think it's longer?

See if, in any part of these two scenarios, there is irrefutable evidence to support either theory. If not, why not? If so, why, what is the evidence?

Put this exercise away for a day or two, then re-read it. How do you feel this time as you go through the lists?

Finally, decide which lists feel more genuine to you. Destroy the other one. It is not important at this juncture whether it is the negative or the positive list that you keep. You are only beginning a journey. Knowing the beginning point is critical. We can only begin where we are.

— — —

You are where you are because this is where you are. This can be seen as both bad news and good news. Most of what holds any of us back is the stories we tell ourselves. The downside is that, well, the stories we tell ourselves are what hold us back. The better news is that if we don't like our story, we get to re-write it.

This is a reason to celebrate, don't you agree?

Chapter 3

INTUITION: REVEALING
THE TRUTH OF WHAT
WE ALREADY KNOW

*"I want to be with those who
know secret things or else alone."*
—Rainer Maria Rilke

o you ever sit in a coffee shop or an airport and people-watch, imagining what their lives are like; quietly creating your version of their life based on how they're dressed or carry themselves? Do you write stories about those you observe, or make quick mental notes perhaps to use something you have observed in your writings? Do you allow that creative nagging voice a temporary stage, indulging – even if only for a moment – a passion to tell a story?

As an attorney, you have been trained to observe everything about everyone, always. You couldn't turn off those powers of

29

observation even if you wanted to. Since law school they have become a part of you, like dark hair and blue eyes. Like in a poker game, you use these skills to your advantage in your career by holding your own hand close to your chest while watching how your fellow players move, draw, or twitch their eyes. And the entire time you are creating scenarios in your head.

When you prep your clients for a deposition or trial, you take all things into consideration, including how they look, move, talk, behave, react, or don't react. In an effort to prepare your clients for interrogation, you basically rehearse possibilities and responses you would like to have. You guide them in how to handle questions and how to tell the truth without over telling or over sharing something that might hurt the case. You direct them in how to dress for court. You coach them on how to sit and tell them not to fidget or react to whatever is going on in the witness box. You give them guidelines for appropriate courtroom etiquette. Your cases and the well-being of your clients require you to create a world, a stage, where all the scenes are pre-viewed beforehand. In other words, you tell stories every day. Albeit true stories, but your version, or your client's – the facts behind the story that best prove what you want to convey.

Perhaps you never thought of what you do as an attorney that way before now. You never noticed the very intricate dance you could probably perform while sleepwalking, because you have done it so often. It has become second nature, instinctive.

But think back to your first case, the first one you tried as lead attorney. That instinct had not been honed yet. Still, intuitively your gut told you what you needed to do. Yes, perhaps there were butterflies or doubts, but you knew instinctively what you needed to portray to the jury or to opposing counsel in order to achieve your goal of justice or compensation for an injustice or error that had been committed.

That same intuitive factor is at work when you write. Combine that with the individual story each one of your cases invites you into. You write because it is who you are. All the things that made law a perfect career for you can help you with your writing. They are still inside of you, asking to come out and help you write.

You write because you can't not write. Your intuition or your gut or, as the Merriam-Webster Dictionary states, "something that is known or understood without proof of evidence" simply won't allow you *not* to write. The question becomes why aren't you writing or, if you are writing, why aren't you finishing it?

Do the voices of your characters wake you up at night, asking you to tell their story? Do you hear their voices and discount them as insignificant, or do you allow them to come out and play?

— — —

I had a pretty bad fall a little over a year ago. I was picked up in an ambulance at a restaurant on a Thursday night and on Friday morning I was being operated on. My kneecap was shattered into several pieces, requiring they not only put two screws in it (seriously, like the kind from Home Depot) but also that they pull the pieces together by wrapping wire around the kneecap three times and closing it with a bolt. I was in a leg brace, unable to put pressure on my knee or bend it for almost two months. And because it was my right leg, I was unable to drive for almost four months. I had to learn to re-bend my knee – not a process I prescribe for the faint of heart. My point is that I had to stop what I had been doing in my life. My life, as I knew it anyway, came to a screeching halt for four months... and it was the loveliest time I can remember apart from the birth of my son.

Why? Because I had to stop moving and just *be* – be with my thoughts, my desires, my demons, and myself. I couldn't walk, couldn't drive, and was completely dependent on others, which was not a feeling I relished. I bet you wouldn't, either. But it was what allowed me to truly listen to the voices that had been there patiently waiting for my attention. Before you send the men in the little white coats, ask yourself if you know the voices I'm talking about. You do, don't you?

I can't know what your life is like, but my guess is that it is filled with activity. You have so many things pulling on you and you rarely stop to question the order in which you do things. Your day begins and you just respond. Your calendar is booked up months out, and you plan accordingly. But what is it inside that is begging to be heard over the noise? What part of you is left outside in the dark, while the practical, logical, rational, and responsible you go through the days?

I want to help you find that part of yourself that you keep under wraps. This is where we are going to begin to examine the truth about writing your book and look at the desire that keeps popping up for you in the most inconvenient places and times.

Now is when you will begin to understand how critical and vital intuition is, why it won't let us quit on our dreams, and what it does when we try.

> *"Is that all there is?"*
> **—Peggy Lee**

The song "Is That All There Is?" made popular by Peggy Lee, recounts a series of devastating events, beginning with a fire when she was a child, and going through the disappointment of a circus and then a broken heart after being jilted. The song is obviously rather melancholic and the last stanza asks why, if life is such a disappointment, shouldn't she just end it all. Poetically, the response is that she doesn't because she knows death will be just as disappointing.

That phrase "Is that all there is?" became a widely used expression, and it's still in fashion today. It was a question way before Peggy Lee immortalized it. It is the question we ask ourselves after we have climbed to a great peak only to discover that the thrill was in the climb, not the achievement. It is the angst we feel when we look back at choices we made and wonder what life would have held if we had taken the other path. It is what happens when we ignore that "still small voice" within us.

You chose a career in law for one or more of many reasons – financial, family heritage, default, prestige, imagined freedom, esteem of the branch of government. I could go on, but you know your reasons. And yet, despite all of the good reasons you had then and continue with today, you still ask yourself, "Is that all there is?"

Well, is it?

I hope you answered no, because it doesn't have to be. If you have made it this far in the book, my guess is that you don't want it to be.

What if we started today to uncover and remove some of the obstacles standing between you and the novel you long to write and finish?

What if the voices of your characters were truly allowed a place in your life, a time when you sat with them and listened to what they want to tell you? What if you invited them out for a glass of wine to talk about all the things going on in their lives? How would it feel to "hang out" with the characters in your book, to have dinner with them, laugh over a shared joke with them, talk about the day – yours and theirs?

I am imagining that would be a blast for them, and for you too. For so long you have tried to quell the voices inside. You have worked so hard to get where you are, and so much depends on you maintaining and doing a good job, but that nagging sensation is still there and it still asks, "Is that all there is?"

Guess what? Your characters are doing the same thing. They are wondering why you only pull them out occasionally, squeezing them into a corner of your life when you have a few extra minutes, instead of truly giving them the space to grow. They are asking you, "Is that all there is?" What would you like to tell them? What would you like to answer for your own life?

What if you made a conscious choice today to honor that deep part of you that longs to be expressed? What if you answered, "No, that's *not* all there is," and set about living that fuller life? How would that feel?

If this evokes a feeling of joy, excitement, and panic, that is okay. This process is like the journey a butterfly has to make to free itself from the cocoon – tedious, perhaps; challenging at best; difficult at worst, but so worth it in the end.

Let's get started, shall we?

Cliff Diving: Picking up the Pen

Here is a great quote by Anaïs Nin: "And then the day came when the risk to remain tight in a bud was greater than the risk it took to bloom." I love this quote because she is acknowledging that there is risk in either scenario.

We assume that there is risk when we step into our dreams – take the leap, so to speak – praying all the way down that there is a net at the bottom so that the fall will be softened. But often we forget that there is also a risk in not jumping. We deny the obvious because it is so close to us we can't see it.

Not writing is a risk. Sure, it's a less noticeable one, but it's a risk just the same. It's the risk that the better parts of who we are will dry up and become non-existent and, in the process of risking that, the pain of our denial turn us into less than ourselves.

But that is not who you truly are. You are ready to bloom. As scary as it may seem, picking up that pen or turning on the computer to write are the safest things you can do for self-preservation. And that is what you are about to do right now.

If you have been following along and doing the exercises in each chapter, you have been doing 15 minutes of free form writing each morning. You may or may not have been doing daily or periodic journal entries, depending on your own needs and desires. The purpose of these exercises is to begin to free you from the prison of doubt and dread; to bring play into the writing process. All day long you write out of obligation. Your documents are court-ordered, very precise. Everything is decided for you to keep order and format in the system. You are told what font to use, what point size and indentions, margins, headings, citations – all of it. In the free-form writing I ask you to do – which includes turning the paper or journal in the landscape direction and writing on paper without lines or guidelines – the only rule is to write non-stop for 15 minutes. The idea behind writing with the paper in a landscape direction and without lines is that by eliminating all known guidelines for writing, you send a signal to your right brain, your creative brain, that it can come out and play. You are inviting it to the playground for a spin on a merry-go-round.

The reason I initially set the time to 15 minutes is because, due to the nature of your legal writings, 15 minutes of freewriting was most likely all your brain could process at the beginning, without going into panic mode. My hope for you is that as you have continued the practice, you have found greater ease and enjoyment in doing the exercise. Perhaps you have extended the time to 20 minutes, or maybe even 30. If not, and you wish to do so beginning with this chapter, please do.

But what I hope most for you is that you have found a sense of fun and adventure in writing again. Inviting your author ego out for a play date encourages her to visit more often. You may have noticed an awakening in your creativity, maybe in the form of a greater desire to write more often or for longer periods of time.

In Chapter 1, we played with future tripping – writing your story from a place of future accomplishment. You took a few minutes to daydream about what your life would look like as a *New York Times* bestselling author.

What was that like? Was it an easy exercise, or did you find yourself needing to repeat it to fully embrace it? Remember that there is no right way to do the exercise. One way is not better than another; they are just representative of where we are at the moment. It is critical that you don't bombard your inner voice with demands to appear a certain way at a certain time. The more you coax the voice out, the more fun you make the process, the more often it will show up and the easier it will be to access it, to access who you truly are inside. Be patient and just observe what comes up for you when you do your daily free-form writing and any of the exercises in the book.

Have fun with this writing. When you notice an urge to write, then write. Honor your muse. Break out the pen or the computer. Write for as long as the words flow, allowing them to come out with joy and ease.

Afterward, make yourself a special cup of tea or a coffee with Bailey's Irish Cream.

Later, if time permits, take your muse for a walk to a special place, like a botanical garden. Buy her flowers. Take her to explore your local art museum or a funky boho coffee or dress shop. Buy some crayons and an adult coloring book. Turn on music, light a candle, and dance around the house. Do anything that invites joy into your life. It will support your writing. Take the time to let your feelings sink in as you do something special, even if it's just looking in the mirror and smiling back at yourself. Embrace and cherish the time spend writing.

By spending time with your author ego, your muse, you will get to know her. Allow yourself to love her without expectations and she will begin to show up more and more often.

Exercise for Enlightenment – Play with Your Story

Begin to think about your novel. Perhaps you are already halfway through it and find yourself stuck. Maybe you haven't started yet, or have started and abandoned it in frustration. Wherever you are in the process, *you are exactly where you need to be*. It is no accident that you are here now, reading this.

Part 1:

For this exercise, use either a stack of index cards or several sheets of blank copy paper (turned horizontally) and write out one concept of your story. For example, if it is a mystery, you could jot down who dies, who discovers the body, who is accused, who has something to hide. If it is a love story, does the heroine begin with a broken heart? Has she sworn off men? If it is a political thriller, who is hiding what? What are the consequences?

Think of where your hero or heroine begins and where you want them to end up. Spend at least 45 minutes thinking through your novel, and let your characters guide you. If this becomes stressful, take a ten-minute break, go outside, color in your new coloring book, make some tea, or do a few yoga poses. Do something to help you relax.

Then, before you begin again, sit comfortably and close your eyes for a minute. Breathe deeply, without holding in your stomach, allowing your diaphragm to rise and fall easily, encouraging your exhale to be longer than your inhale. Imagine all the stress in your body running down your arms like raindrops down a windowpane. Once you feel a bit more at peace, take a look once more at the concept for your novel. What does your character want to accomplish in this story? Does she need help? If so, who can or will help her? What obstacles will she have to overcome? Will she fail or triumph?

You are telling only one of her stories for now, in this exercise – only one or a few of the concepts that make up the novel. She may have many she wants to tell you, but let this one first concept fall out gently onto the index card or paper.

After 45 minutes, if you feel you are finished, even if you have not finished all the ideas for your book, put it all away and celebrate. This was awesome!

You can come back to this exercise tomorrow or this weekend.

Writing a novel is a dream you have had for a long time. It's okay to take it one step at a time.

You will get this done, but it helps to take all the "shoulds" out of the process to begin with, and just play.

Part 2:
Spend a minimum of 15 minutes describing the two or three main characters in your novel. Who are they? Male? Female?

What ages are they? What do they look like? Where do they live? Do they have families? Do they talk to you? If so, what do they say? What do they want you to know? What are their names? What parts of their stories do they want to tell?

If you find yourself really enjoying it and are on a roll, stay with this exercise. Afterward, write one sentence for each character – something you did not know before this exercise that your character told you; something that perhaps surprised you.

Repeat these exercises when you feel your characters pulling you to listen to them.

— — —

You have done a lot of great work here. Pat yourself on the back and dance a little jig. There is more that you can do to support yourself to write the novel that has been pushing at you, and now you know it. You have invited your author ego to come out and play. And you have allowed yourself to answer yes to the question "Is there is more?"

I hope you feel as much joy for yourself as I feel for you.

Chapter 4

AFTER THE
THRILL IS GONE

"Making art may feel like telling a family secret. 'What will they think of me?'"
—Julia Cameron

opefully you have been able to freewrite every morning. You did the future-author exercise, and you can actually see yourself on a promotional tour. You're feeling pretty good about your progress. So good, in fact, that you decide to share it with a friend over dinner one night.

What happens when you do that? Well, there are a few possibilities. Either your friend is excited for you and wants to know everything about your book. Or your friend tries to "save you from heartache" by gently but kindly discouraging you.

It is perfectly natural for us to want to share our lives with those we care about; those we believe care for us. You, however, have just created a new peace between your desires and your intentions. Up to this point, you were in limbo and you kept your characters locked away in a file drawer. You have only recently opened the drawer. You timidly took that first tricky step onto the bridge of authorship. Seeking feedback from someone not trained to help you cross that tenuous bridge might not be the most supportive thing you can do for yourself.

Consider this possibility: your friend seems skeptical and – with a less than supportive expression – begins to ask questions. Only they don't feel like questions. They feel more like an interrogation. Defensiveness begins to saddle up next to you. You try to blow it off. *This is my friend*, you tell yourself. And yet, every instinct you possess as an attorney is piqued and ready to respond to her questions, as if you are on the witness stand.

As artists, we are naturally drawn to other artists, whether we declare ourselves to the world as an artist or not Sometimes, when we begin to be true to ourselves, a door opens inside us and light spills out on everything else around us. We may begin to see our friends or loved ones in different ways. They may begin to see us differently, and even accuse of not caring for them as we used to.

If we entertain a thought such as "If I write my book, I will lose all my friends," fear and doubt about what we are doing can creep in, because we may begin to equate *movement* with *loss*. A knee-jerk reaction then may be to minimize or downplay what we are doing. In that way, even if we do mention our new creativity, we tack on comments meant to put whomever we're talking to at ease.

By keeping our dreams and ourselves small and undeclared, we think we're protecting our relationships and ourselves from whatever negatives may befall us as we pursue our creative goals. Believing we have to choose between being who we are called to be and losing loved ones can be a very bitter pill to swallow. As artists, what we need most is support and encouragement to let our true talents flourish and blossom. Sadly, we may find that we cannot get that support from friends or family. The support you truly need to continue to follow your dreams initially may need to come from sources outside your circle of family and friends.

— — —

I have a client who was highly successful in the corporate world – she earned a six-figure income, managed over 1000 people, and was the go-to person for getting things fixed or back on track. A few years ago, she decided she wanted a different life, so she consciously chose to have what she called "a year of being uncomfortable." For her, that meant leaving her safe, lucrative job for a consulting position, and telling the world her story.

The interesting thing that happened as a side movement was that she broke up with her significant other of five years. That had not been in her original plan. They had previously discussed marriage at length, yet she realized, as she went through all the upheaval in transitioning her professional life, that her personal life was no longer working for her either.

The things she had believed about her partner being a great guy, and the stories she had told herself about not wanting more, were suddenly revealed for what they had become: stories. What began as a professional evolution to have more time at home with her children evolved into her becoming a completely whole person, by being honest with herself (and her partner) about who she was and what she wanted. She discovered that, in order to follow the dreams she felt called to follow, she had to reexamine all aspects of her life.

No one likes to lose someone they care for or, worse, feel rejected as a result of making different life choices. We often go to great lengths to hold on to a role, or job, friend or loved one, not because it is best for us, but because it is familiar. We often equate *familiar* with *safe* or *good*, when they are neither.

If we begin to associate loss with movement, we may begin to question whether we are actually called to write. Just contemplating the potential loss may frighten us to such a degree we may question that voice we heard, the one that called us to write. We can even begin to doubt that we heard anything at all, imagining our dreams and desires to be frivolous or even inane. These thoughts swirl around in in the vortex of our mind and can potentially create doubt and ambiguity for our project and our beliefs about who we are.

When we start to follow our creative calling, our true calling, we may begin to experience a tug of war between what we know and feel comfortable with and the direction we want to move toward. This is natural. We move through this stage in order to move into anything new. It's a transitional phase. But if we were not expecting it and are not sure how to relate, we can find ourselves wanting to shut down our new creation before it takes flight, in order to keep it from taking a toll on other parts of our lives – parts we never imagined would be affected.

It is much easier, and sometimes even feels safer, to be someone who's working on writing a book, rather than to an author who has written a book. Almost everyone wants to write a book. Being one of the masses that's trying to is far less threatening to our friends and family, particularly our shadow artist friends, than actually doing what's needed to *get it done.*

Thoughts like the ones below carry a big punch, and they can take us dangerously close to quitting our creative endeavor:

- *What will they think of me if I don't show up for _____?*
- *What will _____ think if I don't call her back?*
- *How will I explain what I have been doing with all my free time?*
- *Why I don't go out as much?*

If we don't catch these types of thoughts before they take hold, they have the ability to create feelings that would have us spiraling out of control and lost before we ever truly begin.

Life in the Fast Lane

Before we get too far ahead, let's pause for a moment. We just talked about some things that might give anyone reason to pause, but you are an attorney. Because you have made it your life's blood to weigh the issues and err on the side of winning, you understand the phrase "cut your losses" better than most.

That is part of what you do every day. Vetting with that in mind begins the moment a client walks through your door.

From the initial contact through your decision about whether to take on a case or not, you are weighing the cost benefits against the risk involved. Knowing that this is who you are, it's a reasonable assumption for you to weigh the cost of pursuing your dreams versus the possible fallout of not pursuing them. The good news is that, as we've seen, choosing to follow your dreams is the best risk you can take. Anything else is a sellout – and you are not a sellout. You take risks for the benefit of others every day in your profession. This time, you are choosing to take a risk for yourself.

This risk will pay off, and here is why you can be confident about the journey you are undertaking: as you write the novel you have always dreamed of writing, as you allow your characters to talk to you and tell you their story, you, like my client, begin to evolve into who you were born to be. This may cause some transitional changes in your life and may feel uncomfortable for a while. But – and this is important to remember – friends who deem it in your best interest to "save you" by discouraging you, are simply acting out their own thoughts, doubts, and beliefs. As hard as it may be for you to understand or digest, what they choose to say or not say to you comes from their filters about life and has little, if anything, to do with you.

The good news is that we have the great gift of deciding what we want to take hold of as thought patterns. We can determine whether we stop right now and heed someone's advice to put away our dreams, or whether we keep moving toward our creative goal. We are able to do this because of what we *choose* to tell ourselves, the thoughts we believe about ourselves, and those we choose to believe about our writing and our novel.

What comes up for you surrounding these thoughts?

The Rewrite

As painful as it may be to discover that not everyone wants us to succeed and that some people, surprisingly, may actually want us to fail, there is light at the end of the tunnel.

In order to begin to embrace your dreams and recognize the inner muse as your own, you will have to write a new story. A story with the ending you want it to have, not the one that you perhaps drifted into because the pieces fit pretty well and risking seemed too scary.

In order to re-write your story, it helps to know what your story has been.

We all have stories – for everything – whether we are aware of it or not. We have a story for who we are, another one for why we do what we do, and more for why we can't do what we say we want to do. We also have a story that keeps us – happily or unhappily – exactly where we are now.

The question to ask yourself is: "Is this where I want to be?" If the answer is, "No," then let's get busy on the re-write.

— — —

I'm going to tell you a short story. Go through it and circle all the *facts* you find. Clearly, you understand the term "fact" better than 99% of the population, so this will be an easy, fun exercise. Here's the story:

Charlene has a job as a waitress. She works one regular shift and then she also works a double shift every Saturday, because the tips are better. She is always tired and never has any money. She thought about going back to college and finishing her degree, but says she never has enough time because she works all the time. She says she has no friends, due to her lack of time and energy. But what's most poignant for Charlene is that she believes there is no way out for her, that there is no way to change what she is convinced are her limiting circumstances.

What facts did you find?
These are the facts about Charlene's story:

• She has a job as a waitress.
• She works one regular shift and also a double every Saturday.

Everything else is a story about what Charlene *believes* to be true. The story she tells herself is that she works all the time and because she does she is unable to do anything to make her life better. As a result of that *thought*, she *feels* hopeless and *believes* she has no friends. She is confident that her life will never change.

As long as that remains Charlene's story, she is right – her life won't change. As painful, and perhaps even unkind, as it may seem to say this about Charlene, she can't move away from where she is until she first sees her story as a story rather than as facts.

— — —

I have a client who experiences life much as Charlene does. She feels that the external circumstances of her life keep her stuck in a place she doesn't want to be and that keeps her from living her true life. The truth is that she can't write her story or move into a happier place until she understands that it is her *story* about the circumstances in her life that is keeping her stuck.

Although the people in our circle of friends and family can definitely affect us, they can't write our stories for us. Only we can decide what story we want to write about in our novel, and what story we want our lives to tell. *We* decide, not someone else.

We are constantly moving, either forward or backward, but we are never standing still. Moving forward can seem very daunting at times. Unless we receive the blessings of others, it may even feel as if we are moving against the grain. We don't want to think of ourselves as leaving others behind. There is a true grieving process that can be brought forward by becoming more true to ourselves, especially if we feel a loss as a result of our progress. We may feel guilt in addition to sadness. We may even create an entire story around why it's better to stay where we are.

This is where we have to sift through the story we are telling ourselves about our relationships to determine how much is fact and how much is thought, belief, and story.

When friends tell us they don't believe we care about them anymore because we are always busy, we can check inside and ask ourselves what part of that is truth, what part is fact, and what part is a story?

You have a desire to write your book because it was woven into your DNA. You don't have to listen to that desire. You don't have to follow it. You have a very respectable career, doing good work that you are good at. There is no gun at your head forcing you to write, and yet you can't let it go. You may have tried already. You may come up with a million reasons not to write, but it may be that your dream never lets go of you, even when you try to walk away from it.

Many people do try, however. Many choose to walk a path of least resistance. They move along the course they began many years ago. As they travel that road, if they become overly dissatisfied, they may substitute their longings for writing fiction with more success in business or with financial gain; or they may choose temporary "fixes," such as food, alcohol, shopping, or exercising.

That happens when we try to ignore the inner voice that cries out to be fulfilled. We feel that pain and attempt to fill the wound with something, anything. The sad facts surrounding this are that we each have the ability within us to walk our own path without self-destruction. We have the power to change our thoughts, which allows us to challenge and change our beliefs. We can rewrite our stories, which creates a beautiful ripple effect that touches everyone around us.

> *"Don't you know yet? It is your light,*
> *that lights the world."*
> **—Rumi**

Exercise for Enlightenment –
The Stories We Tell Ourselves

Let's take an honest look at some of the stories we tell ourselves. Some of our stories may be serving us well. But some could be holding us back.

Part 1:

Take roughly 20 minutes and write about why you feel it is a bad idea to write your novel. Do it as a fishing expedition to find your stories.

After you finish, go through and, much like you did with Charlene's story, circle all of the facts – just the facts. What do you come up with?

Next, take roughly 20 minutes to write about why you feel compelled to write your novel. If you can't come up with anything to begin with, that is okay – just start writing anything. With one exception: don't write, "I don't know." That would signal your brain to hide the truth from you. Instead, you can write, "If I did know why I was writing what would it be?"

When you finish both stories, put them down and walk away for at least 24 hours. After 24 hours come back and reread what you wrote. Which story resonates more with you?

Hopefully the story that rings true is the one about what compels you. In the story you want to choose to follow, perhaps you will find a sentence or two to adopt as a mantra that you can use whenever you feel that a false story is encroaching on the true one about your desire to write. This could be something as simple as the phrase "Because I have wanted to do this all my life." Or, it might be as profound as, "I know this story will change peoples lives."

Whatever rings truest for you, take one nugget from the story you want to hold on to and keep it close to you whenever you write.

Part 2:

This is where you get to look at your calendar and tell a realistic story of how much time you can invest in writing your novel. This is not a race, so there is no pressure to write 15 or 20 hours a week. The point here is simply to establish regular "play date" time to invite your muse, your author ego, to show up.

By actually blocking off time in your calendar, you are making a commitment to yourself and telling your brain that writing your story is every bit as important as the work you do as an attorney. You are making an appointment with yourself to accomplish something that means a great deal to you.

The amount of time you want to set aside is up to you. But do make a truthful observation of your calendar and treat this time as sacred. Make the commitment not to break your appointments with your writing unless there's a true emergency.

— — —

Taking the steps toward becoming the artist you are inside is not for the faint of heart. The journey can be arduous, threatening, and full of pitfalls and possibly loss, but being true to who you are is the greatest journey you can undertake. Kudos to you for stepping onto the path.

Chapter 5

THE MERRY-GO-ROUND OF FEAR

*"There is no greater agony than
bearing an untold story inside you."*
—Maya Angelou

ear. When you think of fear, what pops up for you? Spiders, deadlines, not winning the case for your client?

That may have been too easy a question to answer. We all have certain fears we are quick to name off the top of our heads. Mine is sharks, for example.

Fears like of spiders or sharks, we can easily make fun of. Other fears are not defined or disposed of as quickly.

As an attorney, you are under a great deal of pressure to perform. You perform for your clients. You perform for the jury during a trial. You perform for your peers, for the judge, for the witnesses you call. From the moment you enter a courtroom, a part of you has to be "on" at all times, much like a rock star during a concert or a politician who's running for office. Winning a legal battle requires a degree of posturing, bluffing, and daring. Every case you take on has the potential to serve justice to the party wronged, and reveal deception, partisanship, illegality, prejudice, or bias. The list could go on.

Additionally, one missed deadline, one unanswered request for admissions on time, and your case can go sailing out the window.

Not only do you have your client to advocate for, you have to contend with the jockeying of your legal opponent, who may attempt to cover you in paperwork in order to stall.

And then there is the statute of limitations.

But I am not telling you anything you don't live with every day.

A part of you may enjoy the strategy of keeping the game viable. You are, after all, quite capable. I refer to what you do as a game because it can be much like chess – you make your move and wait to see how your opponent reacts, then calculate and move again.

But sometimes the game is draining and grueling. Sometimes there is more at stake and it feels far more like issues of life or death, literally. What do you do with the fear that you might lose? Do you bury it under bravado or more research? Do you work harder and push your way through?

Those thoughts about how you get the job done and how you operate under pressure that come up in your career are also, most likely, the same ones that come up when you write or attempt to write. It may seem that, since the two situations are vastly different, there is no way they could be linked. However, the inner voice that tells us that maybe we aren't good enough, that we should just settle for what we know we can get, that we will never make it past the next roadblock, is the same voice that comes around to tell us we have nothing new to say when we sit down to focus on writing a novel. It tells us it has all been said and done before. It tells us our ideas or our writing style is not up to par. It tells us it would be better for us to just stop now before we hang it all out there and embarrass ourselves or, worse, embarrass our firm or our profession.

That voice of the inner critic is always hanging just around the corner to snag us when we get up to go for a cup of coffee. That critical voice may wear a suit and pretend to be superior, or it may have wings and pretend to be our savior. Either way, under either disguise, this inner critic is a poison that has a way of creeping in so slowly that we are caught unaware. Before you know it, you are having coffee with the man in the suit, and everything he says seems so rational, so logical. Your left-brain kicks in and tosses the right brain and all of her lovely ideas about novel writing to the curb. And then it may be a day or a week or even years before you recognize what has happened.

As a lawyer, you have adopted certain techniques for handling this type of fear, your inner critic, when it comes to your legal career – because you've had to. You can do the same thing for your novel and your characters. You can use the same techniques to stay in the game. You can give your dreams of writing the same advocacy you give your clients. You can fight for them with the same confidence and fervor.

What if you told the inner critic that you were done meeting with him and then you turned around and walked away, left him standing there in his Armani suit with a shocked look on his face, and went back to your desk to finish the chapter in your novel you have been working on?

Where Is All of This Coming from, Anyway?

Fear is an emotion that originates with a thought. All of our emotions begin with a thought. We often want our emotions to be attributable to influences beyond our control, because then we are off the hook of taking responsibility for them. It is hard to hear that we create our own fear; that we are the ones who stop our forward progress. It can be challenging to know that we can write our novel, get it published, and put it out into the world – because, if we can, then why haven't we?

A year ago, as I mentioned earlier, I fell and shattered my knee. Being in a leg brace from ankle to hip, unable to walk, drive, or even shower alone opened a whole new world for me. It highlighted things in my life that needed to change. As a result, I broke off an engagement. Prior to the accident, I was headed down a path that I knew was not my path, but I was allowing all the rational thoughts of the inner critic to convince me it was. And he was very convincing. My inner critic knew where all my buttons were and how to push them. I didn't just sit down for a cup of coffee with my critic, I shared a whole pot. I allowed the thoughts in my head to move me in a direction that I was not supposed to go in. Why did I do that?

I had forgotten the tools I teach my clients to use when they need to examine a thought and test its validity.

My hope for you is that you don't have to break a bone and become non-ambulatory to learn how to disable the voice of the inner critic.

Learning some of the tools of self-coaching and lining up a friend or accountability partner to check in with is very helpful for this process. Then, when the inner critic shows up, you have someone you trust to be both honest supportive of you in this process.

— — —

In this chapter, we are going to do a little house cleaning. We are going to go over some tools you can use to help get rid of the voice of the inner critic – tools to help you hear your true voice.

Choosing to become an attorney put you on a fairly straight and narrow path. You have many ethical obligations, not only to your clients, but to the courts as well. As an officer of the courts, you are expected to set the bar for exemplary behavior. The reasons for this are obvious, but are the repercussions? Not that it is a bad thing to be a law-abiding citizen (and how much better the world would be if we all were), but take a look at how that training, that mindset has impacted your ability to be the writer you've longed to be.

The rule-following, analytical part of your brain is critical for doing the work you do effectively. Unfortunately, it can become the voice of the inner critic, the aforementioned well-dressed, well-behaved, successful "suit" that pops out of nowhere to squash your best ideas.

Understanding in advance that this guy can and most likely will show up gives you an advantage. Using this knowledge, together we can set up some strategies for his unwelcomed visits.

Begin with the basic understanding that our thoughts are within our control. As much as we may want to believe otherwise sometimes, we do have the final say on who keeps us company mentally.

You have no doubt encountered the voice that tells you writing is a waste of time. What do you do with that voice, that thought, when it speaks up?

For many of us, the instinctive thing to do is hop on a painted pony on the merry-go-round of fear and ride until the music stops. How often we do this depends on how loud the voice is and how strong the characters in our novel fight back, wanting to be heard and brought to life. Taking that ride is exhausting and depleting.

Let's look at a new strategy. It doesn't mean we won't still hop on the merry-go-round occasionally, but maybe the ride won't be as long or as dizzying.

The next time the inner critic shows up, invite him in. Sit down with him for a while and, without assigning any emotion to what he is saying to you, just listen. Keeping the emotion out of the moment can be more difficult than listening – trust me, we have all been on this ride. What you do by acknowledging his presence and what he has to say is begin to separate him from yourself. This gives you more power over what choices to make about your thoughts.

It may be helpful to take out a piece of blank paper and write in longhand exactly what our inner critic is saying to you. This gives you a visual of those thoughts. Write down everything that comes up. Don't stop to edit or question. Just write down those critical thoughts. Get every awful thought out that you can.

Once you have done that, stop for a bit. Take a short stretch break, get up and walk around the room, get another cup of coffee or tea – do whatever gives you a little space from what you have just written down.

Come back in about ten minutes and look at what you wrote. Go through each item and ask one simple question about it: "Is this really true?" If you say, "Yes," then ask, "According to whom?" See if you can answer those questions for each item with total honesty and clarity of thought. You may get emotional when you do this, so be prepared. I wish I could spare you that, but I would be robbing you of a gift if I did.

After you have gone through all the yucky thoughts and decided if any of them were facts, and perhaps after you have had a little cry or thrown some things across the room (hopefully nothing too valuable), sit back down and decide if those are thoughts you would choose for the person you love most in the world.

If you discover you do have thoughts you would want a precious loved one to have about themselves, it may be that the inner critic intended that thought for your growth, as a way of polishing your talents. If, however, you do not find a single thought that you would want someone you love to think about themselves, then ask yourself why you would want to inflict them on yourself? Don't you get enough real life abuse trying to change the world as a hero in the legal arena?

The next time the "suit" shows up with all kinds of critical advice, remember to ask those two questions: "Is it really true?" and "According to whom?"

Nature or Nurture? Real or Imagined?

There is a lot of debate and research about how and when we establish beliefs, and even what a belief actually is. This simple definition, from ChangingMinds.org is that "a belief is an assumed truth." When and how these "assumed truths" are formed is a bit more complicated, but – according to Psychocentral.com; *Developmental Review*, by David Muiwhey,; and the University of Michigan, to name a few sources – we copy and replicate the core beliefs of our caregivers (typically our parents) without awareness until life experiences allow, or force us to allow, for alternatives to our programmed possibilities.

This suggests that much of what we believe to be true came from the belief systems of those who raised us. And because those beliefs began being passed along to us so early in our lives, we have carried them around a long time. They have become very attached to us, and we've become very attached to them. But that doesn't mean we have to keep them.

It isn't always going to be a "pop the cork" kind of celebration to let go of old beliefs that don't serve us. At times, doing so is likely to feel painful, and the process can be bittersweet. But, in order for you to truly begin to live the life you were called to live, you must catch these false thoughts when they appear and politely shoo them on their way.

Got to Go Round

Some days the words fly off your fingers. Your characters are talking to you so fast you can't keep up. Other days, it seems they have gone on an extended vacation and you can't find a single thing to say. The voice of the inner critique may show up again. He has a new suit he wants to show you, a new critical thought. Don't let this throw you into a panic. Any new thought that arrives with the purpose of stopping you from writing is just the same old stuff in a new suit. Take it for what it is. Write it down, ask the two questions, and see what that does; see if that disempowers the thought. If not, it may be that your author ego needs to just go and play that day. Listen to her. She wants to write this novel even more than you do. If she has gone into hiding it may be because she is tired or bored with what you've been doing and wants you to go play with her and reconnect more strongly to the source of your creativity.

A critical component to making room for your author ego to come out, and for getting the "suit" to leave, is not to hide from those thoughts. Remind yourself that those thoughts have likely been with you for a long time, and they may continue walking with you into old age, but they are not something to run away from.

Self-doubt creeps up for all of us, from time to time, often way more frequently than we would like. It is so easy to start judging yourself critically because you feel you have been on this merry-go-round ride before. You've conquered these demons, slain these dragons, but they just keep showing up. Remember to have compassion for yourself when you go round and round. It will make a big difference in slowing the ride enough to step off it again. Having compassion for yourself when critical thoughts show up will help you understand and handle the thoughts and keep them from being so crippling.

Lining up support around this issue can also be a big help. For example, you can look for and find a writing group (through sources like Meet Up or other online resources), enlist a trusted friend, a coach, or a counselor.

Compassion is an important part of supporting yourself and allowing your novel to emerge. As the poet Rumi said, "What you seek is seeking you." All you have to do is let it find you, and it will.

Exercise for Enlightenment – The Ritual of Writing

Are you still continuing the 15-minute morning writing ritual? I hope you are.

With this exercise, you'll now also start writing your novel in earnest.

Taking the cards or papers you wrote earlier of the concepts of your story and place them in the chronological order they will fall into. Also take out the character descriptions from Chapter 3's exercises and, using these two guidelines, start your novel. It is time and you are ready.

You already made time in your calendar to write. You may want to have a special place designated just for writing. You may also find that having some type of ritual lets your author ego know she is being invited out to play. This might be a special tea you drink as you write, or it might be lighting a candle, turning on specific music, closing the door to the room where you write, or wearing a special item of clothing.

Whatever it is that you do to signal to your author ego that you are ready to write, take a few minutes to do that, and then start writing.

— — —

This has been a challenging chapter. You've examined the ways your inner critic confuses you by using invisible walls, ghosts, and fraudulent voices. But you have proven that you are not hiding out anymore. Celebrate this victory. And remember that if you need help, you can reach out to your support group.

> *"You are the Hero of your own story."*
> **—Joseph Campbell**

Chapter 6

COURAGE: HOLDING OUT FOR A HERO

*"Courage is resistance to fear,
mastery of fear, not absence of fear."*
—**Mark Twain**

Many years went into your mastery of law – studying, learning, applying, practicing. It didn't happen overnight. Perhaps that is why it is called a law *practice*.

"Practicing" is an interesting way to think about a career, particularly as it pertains to law. The *Oxford Pocket Dictionary* defines *practice* as "habitual action or performance." You habitually perform your job as an attorney. You practice. You practice every day and you probably have for a decade or two. You may not think much about it when you state, "I have a law practice." How about applying that concept to anything you undertake in your creative endeavors?

Instead of practicing writing a novel, there is an unspoken, unwritten expectation of perfection. How much consideration have you given to the practice of writing your novel? Do you imagine yourself engaging daily with the art of sitting with your thoughts about your novel, then rattling them off into the computer as they pour out of you in sweeping, magical sentences? The story never hits roadblocks and rarely, if ever, gets shredded and thrown into the trash. It is birthed in all of its glory without even the tiniest of labor pains.

Is that the image you have in your mind of this process of writing? Some artists do. Unfortunately, that expectation can lead us to conclude that if our process is less than picture-perfect, if it contains the least bit of hesitancy or reluctance, that means we aren't cut out to write a novel and don't have anything important to say. Otherwise, the mad gremlins tell us, we would never hesitate with our writing, we would experience the continuous pleasure of forming sentences, our naming of characters and telling of the story would be so thrilling and engrossing it would compel us to skip meals, miss meetings, and happily forgo sleep. We would perform with pure passion, and with no need for practice.

It is ironic that we chose a career path unlike that of the starving artist, yet we still seem to imagine that failure awaits us if we try to create art.

Practicing novel writing is a great way to discover more thoughts that may be in your way. One of the most important practices we can develop as artists is learning to recognize our thoughts and emotions and distinguish between those that are motivating or encouraging and those that are designed to stop us cold in our tracks.

When we are "not writing," we can spend hours and untold energy labeling ourselves. We turn our lack of getting started or our procrastination into metaphorical whips with which to self-flagellate. We come up with reason after reason why we can't or shouldn't write and then, once we have thoroughly convinced ourselves of the endeavor's insignificance, we confirm what we suspected about ourselves all along: we just aren't writers. Sure, we can write legal briefs, but we weren't meant to write anything else.

Because of that need to be perfect from the beginning, the aversion to practicing becomes the harbinger of doom. How can we write if every sentence has to be a masterpiece? How can we ever start, or move past the first paragraph, if we fail to understand our thoughts about what we are doing?

What stops us? In a single word: fear. We can call it whatever we like, use any term that fits for us. But in the end, it is the very simple emotion of fear. Simple, and yet so powerful. It may show up in the form of a fear of being rejected or ridiculed, a fear of abandonment, or a fear of being seen as insignificant. Or perhaps as one of our greatest fears, the one we touched on in the last chapter, the fear that we might actually succeed and that it could rock our world. But whether it is the fear of failing or the fear of succeeding, all the hindering thoughts that run through our minds are based on one type of fear or another. As soon as we master one obstacle, it seems there is another there to take its place.

What if we learned to first recognize, then accept and even embrace, this fear instead of trying to run from it at all costs? What if we were able to put an honest label on what keeps us stuck, on the fear that prevents us from writing?

The White Knight Syndrome

There is a part in all of us, including men, which wants to be rescued. Perhaps, for you, that seems reasonable, since, for so many clients, you are the hero in their lives. You are the one charging in to save the day. Without you, your clients would fall victim to whatever malady or inequity life presents to them. You are the one carrying the banner, riding the white horse.

Do you ever wonder when you get to be the one who's rescued? It is a fair question, especially when it comes to your writing. When does it get easier?

Putting our art out there for the world to see and have an opinion about cries for protection. Our characters come to us with their stories – timid, anxious about how we will present them. They are vulnerable, which makes us vulnerable, which creates a modicum of fear. Okay, maybe more than that. We may have buckets of fear. But, guess what? That is perfectly in line with what we are doing. It is perfectly expected, perfectly natural. In a word, it is perfect.

The part of us that wants to create, to write, is the right-brained child who thought eating peanut butter on chicken was acceptable. That child needs to not only be coaxed into coming out to play, but, once out, needs to be protected. Too much cruelty in the form of "helpful" advice, probing questions, or "friendly" criticism sends the creative child back into the cave.

The world can be a frightening place for grown-ups, and our creative endeavor is like a child.

That creative child in us needs to be rescued from the dragons that would slay our dreams. But how? Where is the white knight we dream of? What happens when we toss and turn and no one shows up to rescue us?

So much of yourself is invested in caring for others that you may not have had an opportunity to learn how to be your own hero. When the opposition threatens your clients or loved ones, you know immediately what needs to happen. Because you have invested time practicing defense on behalf of others, you know how to handle those situations – you kick into a systematic, familiar way of dealing with the dangers. There isn't anything they can throw at you that you don't know how to either defend instinctively, or research and strategize a defense for.

But what have you practiced for yourself? What happens when *you* and your creative dreams are threatened? Do you even notice the threats? Or do you react without thought? Do you withdraw? Do you argue? True, you argue for a living, but it is ever done to be your own champion, or is it always in service of others?

Stepping into a role of self-advocacy may seem foreign, and perhaps even like heading into dangerous territory. But this is how you begin to learn how to survive the onslaught of self-doubt that would keep you from becoming the heroine of your own story. This is where you take the term *practice* and learn how to apply it to not only your art, but to your life as well.

In his book *The Icarus Deception*, Seth Godin states: "I don't think the shortage of artists has much to do with the innate ability to create or initiate." For some people, the artistic calling comes in the form of creating a business, designing a house, writing a song, working out a political strategy, or managing a room full of kindergarten students. Artists are not limited to any one medium. The world is wide open for art and creativity in every field of life.

What a tragedy it is, then, that fear creeps in and steals the artist child from its parent. How can we connect with the courage and wonder of our artistic child to help it to fully realize its place in the world? Simply put, we have to recognize our fearful thoughts for what they are: just thoughts.

Limitations live only in our minds."
—Joseph Campbell

Babies are rather fragile, physically, emotionally, and mentally. They depend on their caregivers for everything. Much as a proud parent looks at their infant and believes they could be the next president of the United States, we can look proudly at, protect, defend, and believe in our creative babies, and, even more importantly, in ourselves.

The only way this becomes possible is by first believing it is possible – believing in who we are, believing it is possible that the words we are stringing together will form sentences, believing that those sentences will then form paragraphs, that the paragraphs will form chapters, and that the chapters will tell the story we have carried around. We have to believe it is possible. We have to believe that we, and our creativity, are not happenstance, or luck, or magic. We have to believe our stories, our novels, the voices of our characters cry out to us because they need to be born. We have to believe our characters are not accidents.

We have to believe that writing our story is a natural progression of our growth, much like the way cartilage calcifies into bone. We are born with cartilage which only hardens into bone with the pressure of weight bearing. The interesting thing about the calcification process is that a baby has to fall hundreds of times and continuously pick itself up in order to create the pressure needed to calcify its bones. Without the pressure that comes from practicing, the bones never harden.

The process is much the same for writing our novels. And living our true lives. First, we practice, much like you have practiced law and much like a baby falls and picks itself up. How much practice does it take for a baby to believe she can walk? How much practice did it take for you to believe you could be an attorney? Believing you can stand up and walk is critical to the process. Believing your novel will be written and published is the very same thing.

This is what waiting for the hero is really about. It isn't about a mythological knight racing to protect us from the world. It's about us conquering the dragons that haunt our thoughts and burn our dreams to a crisp with one exhale.

> *"Once I realized that the cold sweat,... wily stalling...*
> *insecurity were part of making art, I was able to relax."*
> **—Seth Godin**

Fear is a part of making art. Fear is part of practicing. Fear is a part of anything we choose to do that encourages us to grow. If you can understand and embrace the idea that the more you move toward your dreams, the more the gremlins will fight to stop you, you will become your own hero.

The process for not letting that fear stop or paralyze you is to know that it will come, to recognize it for what it is, and to practice accepting it. Practice embracing it. Practice moving on in the face of it.

This may require a shift in the way you see things. We shrink and expand in proportion to what we are willing to see, learn, and practice. The shrinking will never take us beyond what we allow. We control how far we want the thought to take us. We can learn to believe in our creations (if we don't already), and we can practice expanding by looking at our thoughts.

We have talked about awareness and resistance. If we are willing to observe our thoughts from a place of non-judgment and curiosity, we will begin to see that what we once labeled *procrastination* or *failure* was just a form of self-doubt, which is a form of fear. If we can begin to develop compassion instead of anger regarding those thoughts, our fears will gradually have less power over us.

Notice that I didn't say that all those fearful thoughts would pack up a camping trailer and go cross-country to visit Yosemite for three months, leaving you alone. They may take some time off, but they will always try to come back. But you get to decide if they can come back into your house or if they have to stay outside in their old ratty trailer (like Chevy Chase's cousins in *National Lampoon's Christmas Vacation*).

How do we decide what thoughts to choose? We begin by observing our thoughts. We take time to become aware of our thoughts. This is a process, a practice of the mind. So we practice.

Science is somewhat divided on how many thoughts the human brain processes every minute. Some sources (like Quora. com) state that the subconscious brain is a super computer that's 80 times more powerful than the conscious brain. The conscious brain averages, according to several sources, between 2500 and 3000 thoughts per hour. That, my friend, is a whole bunch of thoughts. By practicing observation of your own thoughts, you can learn which ones to give your energy to and which ones to ignore. This is done by first becoming aware of how each one affects you.

Many thoughts fly right past us every second without our notice. Others, however – usually the negative thoughts – we play on loops in our minds, going over them from every possible angle. Instead of just looking at those thoughts and recognizing that they are thoughts and, therefore, controllable, we may believe that they are more than that. We may assign power to them and believe that they have power over us. We may even believe that they control us instead of the other way around. And that is where the opportunity for change occurs.

When I suggest that you can change your thoughts, I am not talking about some kind of chicanery; I am talking about true and reliable change. Are you ready for that? Are you ready to stop experiencing the disappointment that occurs when the white knight doesn't ride in?

We initiate this type of change by becoming consciously aware of our *reactions* to our thoughts. That sounds simple enough, right? Try this experiment: when you think about your novel, what is the first thought that pops into your head? Do you smile and imagine the next great discovery your characters are about to embark on? Or do you grimace at the thought of what you have written, or how much you have not written? Does the lecture in your head kick off with, "Why didn't you finish that chapter last night? You are never going to get this written."

Remember that there is no right or wrong when we're reviewing our thoughts. There is only recognition and choice.

Let's start with the first scenario from above. Let's say you are looking forward to the writing appointment you set for yourself tonight. The thought you have is, "This is going to be fun." You are anticipating your writing with openness to hear what your characters have to say.

What emotions might you be experiencing based on those thoughts? Joy and excitement perhaps? Maybe some confidence?

The emotions evoked by your thoughts will prompt you to take an action. If your thoughts create positive emotions, it is more likely that you will approach your writing date with energy and enthusiasm.

Can you see how that one thought triggered a stream of positive emotions that encouraged you to keep your writing appointment and then also possibly gave you new material for your novel as you thought about what your characters might want to say?

Now let's look at the flip side. If you went along the other tack of thought when I asked you to think about your novel, maybe your thought was, "I'm behind on my writing schedule. My characters aren't talking to me. I don't know where to go from here." What feelings come up for you when you think those thoughts? Frustration? Shame? Perhaps you mentally negotiate with yourself.

Mental negotiation is my personal favorite form of compromise: I wrestle with my thoughts. I tell myself I just need some time off. I promise myself I will be more committed in the future. I argue that I have a full-time job and a multitude of other commitments.

But what happens when you or I do this? What is the result?

When we negotiate like this, we set a precedent. The thought that goes off in my head when I wrestle mentally gives me a virtual déjà vu. The voice I hear reminds me of other times I made a commitment to myself and didn't keep it. That same thought then plays like a tired old movie: "Why bother?" Before long, my emotions are in the dumps and feelings of discouragement, disappointment, or failure come along pretty quickly.

What actions do I take when that happens? Very little, I can tell you. I will either tell myself I needed the break – and maybe I truly did – but if I associate not following through with some kind of "I deserve it" mentality, I become defensive that so much is asked of me, even though I'm the one doing the asking, on behalf of my creativity and my dreams. And the end result is the same – due to the way those thoughts made me feel, I am not any more likely to keep my writing time tomorrow because I have proven to myself through my actions that I can't be trusted. I proved my original thought of "You are never going to write this." Ironic, isn't it, how the mind works?

What about you? What happens when you disappoint yourself? What thoughts do you have when you don't keep your commitments to yourself? What feelings come up? What actions do you take as a result of those feelings?

I bet that whatever happens as a result of your feelings proves your original thought. Let me show you more about how this works. I will use myself as an example again. When the circumstance is that I didn't write during my scheduled writing time, the thought that comes up for me is, "No surprise. I do this a lot." With that thought, I experience a feeling of overwhelm or disappointment. Because I don't want to experience those negative feelings, I find a distraction of some kind, like TV, dinner out with a friend, or a glass of wine. The end result is no surprise: I didn't write again.

So how do we change these patterns? First, we notice our thoughts, without judgment. We ask simple questions that invite curiosity, not criticism – questions such as, "I wonder why I didn't keep my writing date?" or "I wonder why it seems like something always happens to distract me just as I am about to begin?" or "I wonder why it seems so much easier to keep other appointments than this one?"

Once we have a clearer picture of the thoughts we have that either support our desires or seem to sabotage them, we can begin to explore them.

A great place to start that exploration is with the simple question "Why?" For example, "Why does it matter if I keep this commitments to myself?" or "What difference does this make if I am only letting myself down?" or "Why am I thinking this way?"

Exercise for Enlightenment – Checking In with Questions

If you are not analytical by nature, you have certainly learned to be that way with the daily practice of law. What might happen if you took 20 minutes to sit with some of the questions that come up when you explore why you have the thoughts you do?

Part 1:

To start, get comfortable. You can put on some relaxing music if you like – whatever makes you most comfortable. Close your eyes. Take several deep breaths and for about five minutes review your body.

Begin with your feet. Imagine your feet completely relaxing and becoming heavy. Wiggle your toes. Notice any restrictions. Move up to your ankles. You can rotate your ankles if you like and if that feels comfortable. Move your attention up your legs and notice if there is any tension in your calves. If so, allow the tension to go. Continue up to your knees. If you are sitting in a position that allows you to stretch your legs straight out in front of you, give it a go. Move on to your thighs, relaxing them as you continue to move your focus up your body.

Tune in to the trunk of your body and notice if there is any tension in your hips or lower back. If so, can you move into a more comfortable position? What are you feeling in your midsection, abdomen, and solar plexus? If you notice something is uncomfortable, what could you do to release it?

Continue this journey on up to your heart, chest, shoulders, neck, and throat. Then move your attention down your arms, allowing them to become heavy. When you move back upward, toward your head, slow your focus down a bit and go through the features of your face, jaw, mouth, cheeks, eyes, and the top of your head – until you have scanned your body from toes to head.

Take three deep breaths, filling your lungs completely and then allowing your exhale to extend longer than your inhale.

What thoughts floated up while you were doing this exercise?

Take a few minutes to write them down.

What *emotions* arose from those thoughts?

Was that a comforting and relaxing exercise for you? Or did it create stress for you? Did you find yourself enjoying it, or did you have the thought that it was a waste of time?

Whatever your thoughts were, *they just were*. They are neither good nor bad. Thoughts are neutral. It is the attachment of emotions to our thoughts that controls the directions we take.

The purpose of this exercise is to allow you to slow down and focus on one event – scanning your body – long enough to become aware of your thoughts and how you feel because of them. This can help you to see that recognizing your thoughts and the ensuing emotions can affect what actions you take.

The joy here is in the process, in the practice of catching thoughts and becoming the director of them, instead of being directed by them.

I suggest that you practice this exercise until it becomes one of habitual relaxation and awareness. Why? Because it will be a quick five minute journey you can take if you find yourself caught up in a maelstrom of thoughts or feelings. When you feel you are losing the battle with whatever the world has presented, you can stop, close your eyes, and check in with yourself. What are your thoughts? What thoughts do you choose to keep?

Part 2:

Take about 20 minutes to make a list of ten (or more, if you have them) things you want concerning your book. Swing for the fence. Get very clean and specific about your desires surrounding your book. Don't hold back. Dream here. What do you really, *really* want? To prove something to yourself? To prove something to someone else? To earn the respect of someone? To make money? To eventually change careers? What are you hoping for the outcome of having written a book?

After you have written your list, go back and insert between every other item something that you already have. It can be something regarding your book or your life. For example, you may have wanted to become a successful attorney, at one point, and now you have done that. You may have wanted to own a home, and now you do.

The objective here is to make a list of what you truly want and intersperse those wants with goals you have already achieved. We are inserting current success into future dreams. Things we have now were most likely goals, intentions, and desires at one point. By recognizing that we have met many of our goals already, we can begin to more easily allow ourselves to dream from a place of fullness, not lack. This allows us to see that not everything we want is beyond us. We see that we are capable of making our dreams come true – because we've already done so.

Notice what thoughts come up for you while doing this exercise. Do they encourage you to move forward or to stop?

— — —

This chapter is about practicing becoming your own hero. Recognize your progress. Acknowledge the work you have done and how far you have come.

> *"Limitations live only in our minds. But if we use our imaginations, our possibilities become limitless."*
> **—Joseph Campbell**

Chapter 7

TAKING ACTION

"Action is the foundational key to success."
—Pablo Picasso

*a*ction – the word a director uses to cue the camera to begin rolling on a new scene. As you've been making progress with your book, you have been in a new scene. Hopefully, you have put writing time in your calendar and are in the throes of having a blast with your characters and your story. If you aren't as far along as you might like to be, remember that often a single scene in a movie requires dozens of takes before it's done.

Life is like that, too. We get the chance to call "Action!" every time we pick up the pen or open the computer. Much like with the prep work you do for a case, there may be stumbling blocks along the path. The journey isn't always covered in soft green moss. There isn't always blue sky.

If you're still reading this book, you have likely found some inspiration and encouragement regarding your dream. You know by now that the inner critic will visit as often as he can, in any form he can take on, and that might throw you off your game.

The purpose of this chapter is to really drill down to some basic practices and helpful tools to keep you rocking along, even when the critic comes calling. We are going to fill your toolbox with enough good stuff to allow you to give the critic the finger so you can go out dancing with your characters.

The Journey of 1,000 Miles Begins with One Step

Have you given any thought to when you would like to be finished with your novel? This question may sound a bit counter intuitive. You may not have begun writing with an end in mind for your story, much less an end date for being finished writing it. But what happens when you hit the proverbial writer's block? Do your characters just stop in the middle of a scene, turn to you and say, "Now what?" We have talked about some ways to invite your inner author back out to play. If it happens repeatedly and you find yourself completely stuck, none of the things you have tried may be working.

That is why we are going to reverse the process a bit to help set you up for success.

There is something magical about setting a concrete, immutable goal and writing it down. You have experienced this many times. Perhaps you didn't set the goal initially. It might have been set for you by the courts calendar, by the health of a client, by the availability of an expert witness, or by the demands of other cases you were working on. Whatever the compelling reason, once something goes on your calendar for work it is usually a done deal, unless there are circumstances beyond your control that intervene to change that. Have you made that same type of commitment to your characters? Have you made that same type of commitment to yourself? Have you considered doing that for your book? You can set a date by when you will finish your novel, establish a regular writing time, and treat those commitments with the same sense of duty and obligation you would a case you were working on.

It may seem incongruent to give what you may once have considered a hobby the same priority you do a case. After all, law is your profession. It pays the bills. But writing feeds your soul. They both provide sustenance, albeit in different forms. If you are an artist (and we have established that you are), then food is food, and both forms of nourishment are necessary. The soul food your writing provides nourishes the inner part of you.

So pick a reasonable date by when you commit to finishing your novel. Think about how long you want your novel to be. I know, this is another new concept, and it may seem frightening. But you have the training to do this, too. You write briefs and responses almost every day. The courts may dictate the length and breadth or brevity of what you write. You know that you can flood your opponent with lengthy paperwork. You also know that you can answer what is required with an economy of words, when necessary.

You may be mentally telling me that writing a legal document is hardly the same as writing a novel, which may seem harder to plan a due date for. But isn't it the same? In so many ways, you are constantly writing to persuade. That is your job, and you are very good at it. Why is writing a novel different? You are persuading your reader that your characters have something meaningful to tell them. Your characters are persuading you to tell their story. You are persuading your characters to make it interesting enough to hold the reader rapt.

If you really think about it, you have been practicing for writing this novel your entire legal career. You may not have seen it that way until now. Try seeing it that way now. How would you go about deciding how long to make your novel if you used the same skills you use in your law career? There are internet resources you can use to help you calculate how long you want your novel to be. Do you want it to be a full novel, or a novella? The average number of words in a novella is 30,000. The average number of words in a novel is 70,000. These are just general, average word counts.

Now, if you have already jumped in and used the cards you wrote out for your characters' actions to outline your story, you may have started writing. If you have, you will have a slight advantage here. You can look back and determine how much time you spent writing and what your production turnout was – roughly how many words do you write in an hour? This will give you a great starting point for figuring out timelines for your commitments to finishing your novel.

If you haven't gotten that far yet, there is a little exercise you can do to get some concept of what you are capable of. You can set a timer for 30 minutes and just begin writing. Write free form, in stream of consciousness mode, the way you have hopefully been doing in the mornings. Do not panic if you have nothing to say at first, just start writing. As you get into it, you may find the words begin to flow with more focus. It doesn't matter if what you're writing is part of your story or just a string of words. The idea is that you will have some idea of what you can crank out in 30 minutes.

Once you have determined how much you can generally write in 30 minutes, divide the average number of either a novel or novella by this number and you will have a general idea of how long it will take you to write your book. Surprised?

Take out your calendar and look at the time you've blocked off as regular times for writing. Remember, this writing is food for your soul. This is just as important as the other things that clamor for your attention on a daily basis. Yes, I know. It doesn't always feel that way. Take a moment to ask yourself why not? What is the thought that comes up when you think about advocating for your dream in the same way you advocate for a client, by scheduling time and defending it so that you follow through? Take a few minutes to work through that thought process. What emotion does that thought bring up? What is your knee-jerk reaction to that emotion? What happens then?

These questions are for your self-exploration. The only crucial requirement here is that you look at your thoughts and the resulting emotions with neutrality or, better yet, kindness. The thought that comes up telling you that your writing is not as important as the other things in your life is probably one you have had for a while. Otherwise, you would most likely have finished your novel by now, right? These may be long-standing thoughts that have turned into beliefs, and understanding that will take you much further along toward dismantling them.

Just look at those thoughts with curiosity. Ask yourself why you might think that. You may come up with a host of what sound like validating reasons. Some of them actually may be. But the majority of them will be self-sabotaging thoughts. The only thing you need to know once you have identified them, is whether they are thoughts you want to keep. Are they taking you where you want to go? If they work for you, great. But, if not, you may want to consider introducing new thoughts. We will do some exercises about new thoughts at the end of this chapter. For now, go ahead and block off times on your calendar when you will feasibly sit down and write.

It may be that you truly don't have but an hour per week. If so, that is okay. But ask yourself if it is true that you only have an hour per week – or is that simply all you want to allocate. Either answer is fine. It is only important that you know the true answer for yourself.

Once you have a general idea of how long it will take you to write your novel, and you have the time set aside on your calendar, you will have the date of when you will finish your novel.

Write down that date in multiple places, perhaps. Set up auto reminders for your writing times. Keep the finished-novel date in front of you as much as possible. When you do that, you are telling your brain that it's a done deal. Remember how the subconscious mind cannot distinguish between reality and imagined reality? You can use this amazing, beautiful, unique gift to your advantage.

I can tell you that this system works. It may seem contrary to creation or creativity. "I mean, don't artists only create when the mood moves them?" you may be asking. Well, yes, some do. But do you know how the ones who accomplish the end goal, a finished creation, and work steadily toward it, even when they don't feel particularly inspired or creative, do it? They practice. Much like you have practiced law for years, artists practice their craft. Sometimes they turn out masterpieces; sometimes it has to go in the garbage. But how do you imagine James Patterson has written 147 novels since 1976? According to Wikipedia, he has had 114 *New York Times* bestselling novels. 67 of them went to #1, which is both a *New York Times* bestseller list record and a Guinness world record. Practice builds competency and confidence.

How do composers like Hans Zimmer, Ludovico Einaudi, or Carter Burwell create beautiful, moving soundtracks within the given parameters of a movie release date? Simple: they practice. They have regular times they work at their craft. And, yes, I realize it is their chosen profession. But again, how is it possible you manage to get the required paperwork to the court on or before the assigned deadline? You prove to yourself practically every day that you have the skills and ability to do this. We are simply transferring them to a different medium, much like a painter may begin to add fibers, paper, or ink to his work, or to paint on objects instead of canvas or wood. It will seem a bit awkward in the beginning, as everything new does. Every new venture requires some period of practice to gain mastery. This is true when learning to cook a new dish or when taking a different way to work. Just be mindful, as you practice, of any thoughts that come up that would deter you. Do this without judgment for the quickest and most beneficial outcome.

Now that you have an end date for the completion of your novel, continue fleshing it all out. If you did the exercises in which you created action scenes for your characters on cards or sheets of paper (see Chapter 3), you have the beginnings of your storyline. If you did not have a chance to do them, that is a great place to start, after you get the end date for your novel.

— — —

Gather the action cards you designed and lay them all out. Look at them for a while until you see or sense a pattern, or storyline. Begin, then, to create some sort of chronological order for the actions of your characters. At that point, you may feel you need to take a break, indulge in the breathing exercise from the last chapter, or just get up and walk around. It is important to be still enough to listen for the voices of your characters. But I have found it helpful to actually get out of my head at this point in the process and do something that involves both moving and mindlessness. This gives your characters the open door they need, and it allows your author ego to emerge.

When you return – after a 30-minute respite, or even after a couple of days – you will be able to see with fresh eyes, hear with openness. You may find your characters have already decided what they want to do when, and all you have to do is line things up sequentially. If this doesn't happen, you may need to sit with them for a while. Look back at the character exercise from Chapter 3. Who are your main characters? What do they want you (and, eventually your readers) to know? Ask them.

Ask your characters to show you how they want their story told. Interview them the way you would a client. Ask them what happens in their story. You may find, as many authors do, that the characters tell you. You may find some of the things you had written down for action scenes are not the direction they want to go in at all. Keep your heart and mind open to changing the direction of the story, if you're lead that way.

Once you have determined the finish date of your book, developed a story line, understood your characters (who they are and what motivates them), established a sequential order for the story, and set up writing times that are non-negotiable, you are ready to begin writing in earnest.

What are your thoughts about this? How do you feel?

A better question might be this one: how do you want to feel? Danielle LaPorte established a booming enterprise based on her book *The Desire Map*. Since the release of her book, LaPorte has developed a workshop template, franchised it, and trained others to guide the process for the masses. Her empire grows daily. Why? She discovered that we all have what she refers to as *core desired feelings*. We operate in the sweet zone, doing whatever it is we do, as long as we maintain those core desired feelings. She has proven that theory to thousands. This is why I ask you how you *want* to feel. Once you know what those desired feelings are for you, you can work backward to determine what thoughts you need to have in order to create those feelings.

Working from a place of joy when you write will go a long way toward helping you write in the zone, in the flow of creativity, regardless of when or how often you write. It will keep your creativity from being a structured obligation. It will keep the practice of writing playful and fun. We are not trying to add more tightly woven structures into your already orderly world. This novel-writing needs to feel more like a play date. Just like a play date, some things can be orderly, but there must also be a lightness and sense of freedom about it. Otherwise, your writing will be less than what it was intended to be.

Your thoughts create your feelings. Your feelings determine what actions you take. These elements in essence determine your creation.

> *"The soul becomes dyed with the color of its thoughts."*
> **—Marcus Aurelius**

What color are your thoughts at this moment? We have gone through a good bit of info. You may be feeling excited about jumping in. Contrarily, you may be feeling overwhelmed. Either state is understandable and perfectly natural. This will be the ebb and flow of your writing world. Just as your legal career has good days and bad days, writing will have its peaks and valleys. It may seem, at times, like you can't hear your muse or your characters. Or you may be hearing quite a lot from them, but life has played fruit-basket-turn-over and you have had to re-order your calendar. You may be frustrated and anxious that the thoughts about your novel will leave you if you can't get to your computer soon. *Relax*. Know that this will happen sometimes. So also will the inner critic in the Armani suit show up to put you down. Or the universe, it seems, creates hurricanes to keep you from writing. Just remember that you can flip the critic off and, after the storm, there is the sun again. Everything moves and changes. Practice is what builds the creative strength that gets you back on track.

> *"A hero is no braver than an ordinary man,*
> *but he is brave five minutes longer."*
> **—Ralph Waldo Emerson**

Don't give up on yourself or your dreams. Hang in there five minutes longer. Establish small daily routines that allow you to write and support your writing. For example, know the best time of day for you to write. Know how long you can write without becoming overly tired or stuck. Keep your thoughts about developing your novel – the ones that come to you at different times of the day as you go about your other activities – in one place, like in a note app on your phone, or in your journal.

Protect your characters, but allow them to be vulnerable.

Be kind to yourself. Have fun. Play.

You will emerge from this project a completely different person than the one who entered it. Be open to change and evolution.

Your characters will do the rest.

Exercise for Enlightenment – Choose to Believe

We have discussed, at length, the link between our thoughts, our emotions, and our actions. Thoughts determine the outcome of our efforts, based on the feelings they evoke.

Discovering the thoughts that are not serving your purpose is foundational to changing your personal story. We have done this work throughout this book. Now we are going to look at this issue from a deeper thought-changing perspective.

List at least three limiting thoughts that come up for you repeatedly. A limiting belief is any thought that causes you to pause or hesitate, even for a moment, in going toward what you truly want.

Write down those repeating, limiting thoughts. Look at them. How can you turn those thoughts around to reflect how you want to feel? Experiment with this for a few minutes. Here's an example. If one of your thoughts is, "I will never finish this book," you could turn that around to be, "I have set an end date for writing my book." Period. It doesn't have to be a flowery, New Age, paragraph-long affirmation. It just has to be a thought your brain believes, can support, and won't argue with.

If you did write out a long, flowing thought, such as, "I know I haven't finished my book yet, but I also know that this time is different. I know I can do it this time, and I will," you'd be fighting with your brain. It is likely your brain will come back with something like, "Oh yeah, why is this time different?" And you're off with negotiating rather than relaxing into a supportive thought. Rather than jumping right back on the limiting-thought loop and re-hashing times in the past that you haven't succeeded, keep it simple. Keep it honest. Keep it believable.

The subconscious does not distinguish between reality and imagination. But if the new thought is not believable, your brain will fight against you in an effort to prove the previous data (those thoughts you entertained until they became beliefs) with even more conviction.

The beauty of this system is that any new thought and/or new behavior based on a repeated, supportive thought that you believe is true, encourages more of the same. This means more time spent writing, or more frequency spent writing, encourages more of the same. The super computer kicks in because the brain has gone through this process before. It knows the drill. The awkwardness of getting started is reduced. This is why having some sort of writing ritual, even something small, can help to trigger the brain to be supportive. The symbolic movement acts like a trigger (much like when I pick up my keys and my dog heads for the front door).

Think back to your first actual case in a courtroom. How much prep went into making that happen? I don't mean the actual legal work. I mean the head work you did. How many times did you evaluate what you were going to wear? How much time was spent checking to make sure you had everything in your briefcase? How many big and little pep talks did you give yourself?

The secret is to practice repeating new thoughts until they become beliefs that support you and your dreams.

> *"Vulnerability is the birthplace of*
> *innovation, creativity and change."*
> **—Brené Brown**

I hope you have found this journey helpful, that you are by now well established in a writing practice, and that you can see in your mind's eye your novel that it's finished, published, and lining the walls of bookstores.

Remember to reach out and ask for help. As a bonus for readers of this book, I have included a fabulous freebie that will support you in your wonderful endeavor. Check it out on the very last page of the book.

Happy writing!

Acknowledgments

I want to first thank my editor, Grace Kerina. Without her encouragement, guidance, and direction, I would not have been able to write this book. She told me when to stop, when to go, when to let go, and when to buckle down and get it done. I can't thank you enough, Grace.

Additionally, I want to thank my sisters, Sherri, Mary Ellen, and Beth. Mary Ellen served as my muse, supporter, additional editor, and my constant sounding board. Sherri was ever present for support and encouragement. Beth kept the family going to allow me the time and energy to write. I love and thank you all.

Thanks to my brother, Jeb, who was always a source of lightness and humor in a crazy and hectic world.

Thanks to my Dad, Jim, and my stepmom, Caroline – their unwavering support is always present.

Thanks to my mom, Bobbie, and my stepfather, Jack – although no longer here with me in body, they were never far in spirit. I miss you.

Thanks to Christian, *mon amour*, whose mysterious belief in my abilities served to keep me motivated. *Merci beaucoup*.

Thanks to my Master Mind group – Lauren, Jennifer, Betsy, and Dan. You guys never stopped cheering me on and supplying energy and laughter for the journey. I adore you all.

Thanks to Jennifer Powers, the amazing lady who coached me through some major growth.

Thanks to my beautiful friend Jodi, who introduced me to coaching at a critical and painful time in my life. I will be forever grateful.

Thanks to Brooke Castillo, who taught me great tools for self-coaching.

I want to acknowledge all of the wonderful people who made this book possible for me. They have been a dream to work with, sensitive to any requests I made, very attentive to detail and completely supporting during this entire process.

A very special thanks to Morgan James Publishing and the CEO, David Hancock. Without your trusting and vision this wouldn't be possible, thank you.

Megan Malone, Managing Editor and superwoman, who keeps all the balls in the air and me on task, thank you.

Jim Howard, Branding Expert and Publishing Director, full of great ideas, input and direction, thanks Jim.

And last, but not least, Bethany Marshall, Assistant Publishing Director and Nickcole Watkins, Senior Marketing Relations Manager. Thank you all for being a safety net and champion of writers.

I am grateful for this team, thank you.

And, last but not least, thanks to Angela Lauria, whose energy, humor, honesty, and creativity are unparalleled. You're the best publisher ever!

ABOUT THE AUTHOR

 Kim Benjamin is a Certified Life Coach, Creativity Coach, author, and successful entrepreneur. She has spent the last 25 years creating and running small businesses while following her own creative muse. She grew up in a family of attorneys, where writing and reading were as essential as eating, so she understands the demands on the life of a busy practicing attorney. She also knows about the great number of stories lawyers have to tell – usually with excellent turns of phrase; stories that are indicative of an urge to write that most attorneys she's met seem to harbor. Kim is passionate about walking with you through the journey to make your writing dreams real.

Kim is currently living in Paris, France – following her own dreams. She is open, available, and eagerly awaiting contact from attorneys just like you, so she can help make more dreams come true.

Thank You

You have taken time out of your very busy life to read this book. I appreciate your investment and want to offer something in return. **Receive additional tools for finishing your novel. Unlock any doors standing between you and your novel.**

To get your tools, go to <u>KimberlyBenjaminCoaching.com</u> and sign up to receive a questionnaire on the best time to write your novel.

Additionally, you will receive a seven-part email course that will take you to that next step to becoming an author. For seven weeks, I will make a personal visit to your email with additional tools, suggestions, and worksheets.

Included in the weekly instruction will be topics such as:

- The importance of dreaming and playing with the characters in your novel
- How to hear the voice of your characters
- How to establish your writing practice
- How to bring the story to life
- You've finished your novel – now what?
- Self-publishing vs. traditional publishing

Morgan James
Speakers Group

We connect Morgan James published
authors with live and online events
and audiences whom will benefit
from their expertise.

Morgan James makes all of our titles available
through the Library for All Charity Organizations.

www.LibraryForAll.org

Printed in the USA
CPSIA information can be obtained
at www.ICGtesting.com
JSHW080000150824
68134JS00020B/2188

9 781683 503194